Museums and Art Galleries

Making Existing Buildings Accessible

Edited by Adrian Cave

Acknowledgements

This guide has been produced by the Centre for Accessible Environments in conjunction with RIBA Publishing

Edited by Adrian Cave RIBA NRAC Consultant

Individual contributors are listed under each project

Sponsored by the Access Audit Corporation Ltd and by Renaissance in the Regions.

The support of the Museums, Libraries and Archives Council is gratefully acknowledged.

Front cover photograph, east wing entrance at the National Gallery © Morley von Sternberg

Published: January 2007

© Centre for Accessible Environments and RIBA Publishing, 2007

ISBN-13 978 1 85946 175 4
ISBN-10 1 85946 175 1
Stock code 58497

Centre for Accessible Environments
70 South Lambeth Road
London SW8 1RL
Tel/textphone: +44 (0)20 7840 0125
Fax: +44 (0)20 7840 5811
Email: info@cae.org.uk
Website: www.cae.org.uk

The Centre for Accessible Environments is a Company Limited by Guarantee registered in England and Wales No 3112684, Registered Charity No 1050820.

RIBA Publishing
15 Bonhill Street
London EC2P 2EA
Tel: +44 (0)20 7496 8300
Fax: +44 (0)20 7374 8200
Email: sales@ribabooks.com
Website: www.ribabookshops.com

RIBA Publishing is part of RIBA Enterprises, a Company Limited by Guarantee registered in England and Wales No 978271.

Designed by Steve Paveley
Printed and bound by Latimer Trend, Plymouth

Foreword

The Access Audit Corporation Ltd.

As the longest established organisation of its kind in the UK and owned, operated, managed and staffed by disabled people, the Access Audit Corporation Limited (AACL) encounter and deal with access issues on a daily basis.

We strive to understand the needs of those most affected by access problems, which is why we positively discriminate in favour of disabled employees – only in this way can we empathise and understand fully the needs of others and rise to the challenges we encounter.

We have a diverse client base from large and small corporations; local charities, services and government to individuals – as a result we have further developed our range of services to include training, charity consultancy, business consultancy and individual advocacy.

We are pleased to be involved with *Museums and Art Galleries: Making Existing Buildings Accessible* and to support the efforts of the Centre for Accessible Environments (CAE) who, under the tireless leadership of Sarah Langton-Lockton, work hard to direct efforts down the path of inclusive design. Our mission as a company closely mirrors the philosophy of the CAE as we work towards an environment which does not need to consider access issues but rather includes them by default.

Devoting personal time to chair local charities, raising £16 million to date for charities across the UK, and providing free advocacy services are just some of the ways in which AACL gives back to the community.

The knowledge and skill of our own architect are essential in finding access solutions that are cost effective for the client yet open doors for those needing them. Museums and art galleries in their role of historian, teacher and exhibitor are among the first to recognise the needs of the entire spectrum of individuals in society despite the constraints of existing buildings.

We are proud to sponsor this publication which we perceive as a milestone in inclusive design throughout our modern society.

Barry Brooks
Managing Director
The Access Audit Corporation Limited

Foreword

Museums, Libraries and Archives Council

The Museums, Libraries and Archives Council (MLA) is proud to be associated with this groundbreaking book from the Centre for Accessible Environments and RIBA Publishing. MLA and its nine regional agencies work in partnership to provide strategic direction and leadership with the aim of transforming museums, libraries and archives for the future. We work to improve people's lives by building knowledge, supporting learning, inspiring creativity and celebrating identity.

Museums and galleries not only welcome large numbers of visits by schools, community groups and members of the general public, but take their collections out into the community through outreach work. As a natural evolution of this work, they have also developed some of the best practice in access for disabled people worldwide. Multi-sensory galleries, touch collections and audio guides, with descriptions for visually impaired people, have all appeared. British Sign Language tours are increasingly being provided for deaf visitors and induction loops at reception desks help welcome visitors who are hard of hearing. The print size of signage is becoming bigger and more user-friendly. More seating is to be found for those who need it. Events for people with learning difficulties are routine. Innovative, online museum collections, described and interpreted for disabled people, have been created. There is a new awareness of representing the hidden histories of disabled people and their contributions to society are being featured in exhibitions. Increasingly, museums and galleries are becoming inclusive spaces for all.

Museums and Art Galleries: Making Existing Buildings Accessible features case-studies from the Renaissance programme, a national initiative managed by MLA to transform museums in the English regions. The Horniman Museum, Colchester Museum and Tyne and Wear Museum, all of which feature in this book, are inspiring examples of how good design can widen access for diverse audiences.

Architects are our partners in designing museum, library and archive services and facilities for people and communities: we need your commitment, skills and creativity. *Museums and Art Galleries: Making Existing Buildings Accessible* is a most welcome addition to MLA's award-winning guidance on how best to provide access for disabled people to this sector. It is a vibrant testimony to the creative design solutions possible when architects engage with the dual challenge of preserving unique historic environments and widening access for all, and makes an important contribution towards a new civility in contemporary design. We hope that it inspires ever more excellence in inclusive architectural design.

Chris Batt
Chief Executive
Museums, Libraries and Archives Council

Contents

Synopsis

This publication reviews 14 museums and art galleries, all of which are in historic buildings where alterations have been made to improve accessibility for disabled people. Six of the schemes are described by members of the project team, and the remaining eight are described with a short project summary.

The main conclusions from this study, as set out on the following pages, include the following.

■ Use as a museum or an art gallery can often be an effective way of ensuring the future viability of a historic building. An analysis of the history of the building and its development can lend itself to appropriate, sympathetic solutions to access issues.

■ Providing step-free entry directly into a historic building may be less intrusive than the installation of an external ramp or wheelchair platform lift up to the front door.

■ Providing the reception area, shop, café and sanitary accommodation in an annex or basement can help to protect the more vulnerable spaces and features of the building, including the original entrance hall, from the pressure of visitor numbers.

■ Variety and choice for visitors, particularly in access to information and exhibits, can be greatly assisted by systematic consultation with user groups.

■ Fully accessible and clearly marked routes, defined as the primary circulation routes, may make other access issues easier to resolve and reduce the need for extensive alterations in other parts of the premises.

Introduction

Museums and art galleries are particularly relevant to studies about designing for accessibility for three main reasons.

First, they are buildings which large numbers of people may wish to visit in order to enjoy or to benefit from the exhibits or information that are available. These visitors will be diverse and include people with a wide range of disabilities. For some of these, a successful visit may be an especially important experience because of the many limitations which they experience in the built environment generally.

Second, many visitors may only come to a particular museum or gallery once in their lifetime, or be there on their first visit. Therefore, they need to be able to find their way into and through the building with the minimum of difficulty, and to be able to obtain access to the exhibits or information in ways which are appropriate to their particular needs.

Third, because many museums and art galleries are in historic buildings, it is important that the qualities of these buildings are not compromised by intrusive measures taken to improve accessibility. Further, because a visit to an art gallery is for most people a visual and aesthetic experience, the quality of this experience should be enhanced in every way, both in the historic parts of the building and in any new spaces or extensions.

This study, therefore, seeks to examine selected museums and art galleries in which access improvements have been designed with care and attention to detail in order to enquire whether some of the innovative or unorthodox design solutions may contribute to the concept of 'inclusive design'. If a design can be seen, in scientific terms, as a hypothesis for a solution to the design brief, it can be sensible to test the hypothesis, not by examining whether the design conforms to the published guidance in the British Standard BS 8300:2001 (Incorporating Amendment No. 1) *Design of buildings and their approaches to meet the needs of disabled people – Code of practice* (BS 8300:2001) or in Approved Document M: *Access to and use of buildings,* 2004 edition, Building Regulations 2000 (AD M), but whether it works reasonably well in practice for the majority of people and, particularly, of disabled people.

It is a premise of the concept of inclusive design that a design achieves its purpose unobtrusively and with the minimum of additional features or gadgets. In other words, that it meets the needs of almost everyone without proclaiming itself to be designed for disabled people. There are many examples in the projects examined in this study where most people would not realise that the ease with which they entered the building, made enquiries at the reception desk and then enjoyed the exhibitions, shop and café was due largely to the fact that the premises had been adapted to meet the needs of disabled people.

The Museums, Libraries and Archives Council appointed the author and the Centre for Accessible Environments (CAE) in 2003 to undertake a study of *Access with Elegance* at six museums and art galleries in England. This study, which was completed in 2004, demonstrated that a great deal of useful experience had been accumulated about the

Inclusive design:

- places people at the heart of the design process
- responds to human diversity and difference
- offers dignity, autonomy and choice
- provides for flexibility in use

process of making these sensitive buildings accessible, that every project had examples of good practice and of innovative solutions, and that much of this experience could be useful or informative for future projects if described and published systematically. This was the genesis of the present publication.

Methodology

The methodology for the *Access with Elegance* study was based on that commonly used for an access audit, using the sequence of a journey into and through the building and its site. A full access audit normally involves the measurement of such features as door widths, steps, gradients, the heights of desks, door handles, switches, vision panels and so on, the force required to open doors, and the levels of illumination in key areas. Because the purpose of this study was to try to identify examples of good or innovative practice in improving accessibility, the visits followed the same journey sequence as for an access audit. Notes and photographs were taken mainly of those features which were particularly significant from an access point of view. It has to be said at the outset that every one of the visits was an enjoyable and stimulating experience and it is hoped that this will be conveyed by the following descriptions and illustrations.

It became apparent very quickly that a thorough process of consultation with disabled people during the planning and design stages of a project to improve accessibility can make a major contribution to the success of the project. Such consultation can be particularly informative when the constraints of the existing building require innovative solutions which can be reviewed with users at the design stage.

A hypothesis of this book is that there are many ways other than those recommended in publications such as BS 8300:2001 and AD M by which the access needs of disabled people can be met. All of the projects in this publication have features which differ from the design guidance provided in the two documents. Many of these features could be described as innovative, but not necessarily successful, and it is important that designs which vary from the guidelines should be carefully monitored in order to assess the extent to which they are, or are not, helpful in providing access for disabled people.

Experience at several of the premises described in the case studies indicates that most disabled people develop considerable skills to compensate for the difficulties which they encounter in the built environment, and that there may be valuable lessons to be learned from this experience. This applies above all to people who have lived with a specific disability for most of their lives. The issue is how to achieve a balance between the cultural and aesthetic qualities of, for example, a museum in an 18th century house, and the access needs of disabled people who may wish to visit the museum in the 21st century.

Designing for everyone

Designing for visually impaired people is one of the most delicate and difficult aspects of designing for improved accessibility, and there are several reasons for this. For example, the needs of people who are blind are easier to define and relate to features such as touch, acoustics, airflow, smell and so on. In general terms, severely visually impaired people need to be able to feel their way around a building, either by using a cane, for which floor surfaces, kerbs and obstacles in circulation routes are very significant, or by using their hand, in which case the handrails and door handles are important. It is worth noting that for a blind person, the quality of the door, the door handle and handrails may be among the main indicators of the quality of a building because these are touched by the hand and fingers. A lightweight, hollow-core door with a flimsy door-handle feels entirely different from a solid timber door which has generous door-handles and is easy to open. Handrails can vary from flat, narrow sections of wrought iron, via metal or nylon covered circular rails, with a diameter of about 50mm, which are easy to hold, to Victorian timber handrails of monumental proportions which convey much about the character of the building, but can be difficult to hold. People who have long experience of a disability may be able to use other senses to obtain information about their environment in ways of which most people are unaware and, of these, hearing and acoustics are particularly important.

One of the many difficulties in designing for visually impaired people is that the conditions which cause impaired vision vary so greatly. For example, levels of lighting which may be helpful to some people can be too bright or too dark for others. However, there are general principles of inclusive design which include the elimination of glare, graded transitions between areas of high and low illumination, and colour schemes with adequate visual contrasts for features such as steps, handrails, doors and doorways. All these measures meet the principles of inclusive design because they are useful for the majority of people. It is also worth noting that just as designing routes for wheelchair users helps people with walking difficulties, families with young children in buggies and people with wheeled suitcases, providing for the general needs of people with impaired vision can be of great assistance to older people, because, with age, the eye becomes slower to respond to changing conditions of illumination.

The considerations in designing for hearing impaired people include reducing the level of background noise, ensuring that visual features such as signs are adequate, and enabling those who need to lip-read, to do so when talking to staff, particularly at the reception desk and in the shop. To achieve this, it is necessary for the faces of the staff to be illuminated without glare. The provision of appropriate hearing enhancement systems is usually advisable or necessary in reception areas and in exhibition spaces where audio information is provided. Where induction loops are provided, it is essential that they are maintained in working order and staff know how to use them. Audio guides, which describe the exhibits, can be particularly helpful for blind people and, when adapted for hearing aids, for those who are hearing impaired. Hand-held British Sign Language (BSL) guides are becoming increasingly common. When they are available, audio guides are likely to be popular with many visitors partly because, unlike written information, they enable exhibits to be studied while receiving the recorded information. This is an example of how assistive technology can help to make information and interpretation more accessible for everyone.

The process of improving accessibility

Nearly all the projects investigated have been through a long period of design and development, most of which had included feasibility studies for alternative options, with evaluation of relative costs, advantages and disadvantages. It is now clear that decisions can be pre-planned in a sequence and there can be great benefits to the process if all parties are aware of the appropriate stage when certain types of design decision will be made. For example, in the outline and scheme design stages (Stages C and D), the main emphasis is likely to be on circulation routes, taking account of public transport, car parking, entrances into the building and internal circulation, with decisions about whether changes in level require ramps or lifts. Those issues which concern wheelchair access and subsequent requirements at changes of level, and for widths of circulation space, are pre-eminent at these stages of a project. Later, the detailed design stages (Stage E onwards) are the time for decisions which affect features such as door handles, floor finishes, WC design, lighting and colours. If all goes well, decisions at and after completion of the works should not involve changes to decisions made earlier, but may include adjustments of furniture, fixtures, lighting and ancillary aids to meet the needs of an individual, usually a member of staff, who has specific needs. It is during these design stages that a user consultation group can be of great assistance to the design team, which may include representatives of the client, access consultant, architect, conservation specialists and other members of the project team.

At Hollytrees Museum, for example, the consultation group included wheelchair users and people with mobility or manual dexterity impairments. Their input contributed greatly to the creativity and relevance of the design. An example of that influence was a decision to change the sloping footpath outside the Museum from loose gravel to a firm asphalt base with a surface of rolled gravel, providing a surface which was sympathetic in appearance for an 18th century house, but much easier to use for disabled people and families with children in pushchairs. However, it was also agreed that although the slope of the land provided natural gradients of about 1:12, steeper than the preferred gradient of 1:15, this should be accepted, and it would not be appropriate to provide handrails along this slope. As with all innovative design solutions, it is prudent to monitor the use of this feature and if serious problems occur, to make appropriate adjustments.

It is understood that no significant problems occurred at Hollytrees. A similar surface treatment has been provided on the flat footpath approaches at Dulwich Picture Gallery, where the visual appearance of the gravel-surfaced path in the historic setting is of great importance.

Legislation and Codes of Practice

The Disability Discrimination Act 1995 (DDA) came into effect in stages, so that by October 2004, service providers were required to make 'reasonable adjustments' to the physical features of the premises from which their services were provided, to overcome physical barriers to access. Such adjustments involve four options for dealing with the physical feature – removing the feature, altering it, finding a means of avoiding it, or providing the service by a reasonable alternative means. This legislation prompted the publication of many good practice guidelines.

The publication in 2001 of BS 8300:2001 was a significant moment in the development of good practice because the recommendations are based on wide-ranging research and therefore have an authority not available to many earlier publications. For almost the first time, this was a document in which nearly all the criteria were measurable, providing an invaluable tool for the auditing of accessibility in existing buildings. It was not new to have guidelines for the gradients and lengths of ramps (although even these guidelines were changed by BS 8300:2001), but BS 8300:2001 also provided measurable criteria, based on research, for such features as the width of doors in various situations, heights and sizes for door handles and handrails, the spaces required for a wheelchair user to turn from corridors to open doors and to pass through the doorway, the force required to open the door, the size of lettering for various functions, and the contrasts of tone and colour between various surfaces. This was a genuine breakthrough because at last people seeking to improve the quality of the environment for disabled people were able to say, not merely that a door was too narrow or too heavy or too difficult to open, but to point out the ways in which the door did not meet the recommended criteria. However, two problems resulted from the wealth of information provided in BS 8300:2001.

The first of these is that many access auditors and consultants have tended to apply the criteria in BS 8300:2001 without adequate understanding of the needs of people, or of the context. In some cases, this has resulted in property owners and managers being advised that, in order to meet the requirements of the DDA, they needed to make such extensive and expensive changes that this tended to make the idea of improving access for disabled people appear unrealistic. In many cases, a significant contribution to making services accessible to disabled people can be achieved by staff training and improved information, at relatively limited cost, with modifications to the built environment being carried out as resources become available.

The second problem resulting from BS 8300:2001 is that it can be interpreted as a set of rules and applied too rigidly, as though the recommendations were the only way to comply with current good practice, although this was explicitly not the intention of the committee which produced the document. The foreword to BS 8300:2001 states that the design recommendations 'are, where relevant, based on user trials and validated desk studies which formed part of a research project commissioned in 1997 and 2001', whereas previously 'the guidance with respect to the access needs of disabled people was incomplete, in some instances contradictory and, on the whole, not based on validated research. During the course of development of this British Standard, however, it has become clear that further research will be necessary into risks and inconvenience in buildings to people with sensory impairments'. The foreword goes on to emphasise that 'in some instances, recommendations are quite specific; in others, they include dimensional ranges. Where dimensions and/or measurements are stated, they are subject to tolerances. Dimensional ranges are intended to provide designers with some flexibility of design solution'.

Building Regulations

Many of the recommendations in BS 8300:2001 were incorporated into the revised AD M, which came into effect in May 2004. Interestingly, and after extensive consultation following the publication of the British Standard in 2001, some of the recommendations were not included in AD M because the understanding of good practice in designing for disabled people had developed during the intervening period. An example is the question of whether there should be tactile warning surfaces at the top and bottom of stairs; although this can be helpful for visually impaired people, tactile paving can be uncomfortable and even hazardous for some people with mobility impairments who prefer a smooth and predictable surface. The generally accepted recommendation at the time of writing is that tactile paving should not be applied as a matter of course, but only in situations where there are not other and adequate indications of the hazard for people who are blind or partially sighted. The principle that improvements to meet the needs of one group of people should not be disadvantageous to others is fundamental to the concept of inclusive design.

Since the completion of some of the projects covered in this publication, access statements have become a significant feature of the process of improving physical access in existing buildings. Access statements are referred to in the 2004 version of AD M and, since May 2004, have been required by many local authorities as part of Building Regulations applications. There are many ways in which access statements can be presented but, to be effective, they should explain in a systematic way the reasons for the decisions taken about accessibility, any constraints of the existing buildings and the relationship between the physical fabric and the management of the building, particularly for entry and for emergency escape. Decisions about the design, or omission, of tactile paving or other features recommended in BS 8300:2001 could be recorded in an access statement for future reference.

Features of accessible museums and art galleries

Attention to the following issues can bring benefits to the majority of visitors.

Clear provision of information

For many people, a visit to a museum or an art gallery begins with an inspection of the website. During the course of this study, all the projects featured have improved their websites in order to provide information about access routes, car parking, opening hours, facilities, special exhibitions and so on. This information can be invaluable in helping people to plan their visits, while at the same time providing information with a choice of formats which are accessible to different people. These adaptations of format may range from enlarged typefaces or images to audio descriptions and commentaries. Websites have become more accessible, with use of plain language, simple and logical navigation and increased flexibility allowing more user control over the website.

External wayfinding

Finding the way easily to a museum or art gallery is an important part of a good visitor experience. Wayfinding includes clear, direct routes and good signage.

Well-signed routes from main roads and public transport, as at the Queen's House, may include colour coded signs and symbols to help everyone to find their way

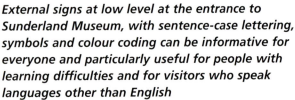

External signs at low level at the entrance to Sunderland Museum, with sentence-case lettering, symbols and colour coding can be informative for everyone and particularly useful for people with learning difficulties and for visitors who speak languages other than English

Designated parking spaces for disabled people at Dulwich Picture Gallery are located conveniently close to the entrance which has a call button at low level

Accessible car parking

Disabled people may be permitted to drive closer to the museum than other visitors, particularly on sloping sites.

Usable footpaths

On steeply sloping sites, it may be impossible to avoid slopes with a gradient of more than 1:20. The illustrations show sloping paths with no handrails, for which the use should be monitored to ensure that there are no serious problems for access. The options may be to provide more handrails plus resting places at intervals of not more than 50m.

A ramp up to the new extension at Horniman Museum, on a steeply sloping site provides an alternative to the long flights of steps up to the original main entrance

© Jonathan Goldberg

As an alternative to traditional gravel paths, rolled gravel on a firm base, at Hollytrees Museum, has a similar appearance but provides easier access for wheelchairs, children's buggies and people with walking difficulties

Step-free access externally

Where change of levels cannot be eliminated or bypassed a combination of a ramp and steps, with handrails on both sides, provides access for everyone.

Portable ramps should normally be seen as a temporary solution to achieving step-free access into buildings because they are always visually intrusive, they do not normally meet the design criteria for independent use and they usually require staff to place, supervise and remove the ramp.

Portable ramps may be useful in the following situations:

- as a temporary solution while other options are being considered

- where funding is not yet available for the construction of an alternative

- in very sensitive locations where any alterations would be undesirable

Step-free entrances

Step-free entry, if necessary with a ramp, is now essential for museums and art galleries. Even radical alterations, such as at the Queen's House, the National Gallery and Hollytrees Museum, can be designed to be sympathetic to the original character of the building.

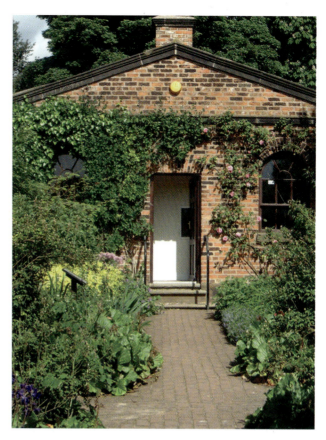

This is the main doorway to a walled garden at Norton Priory. An alternative route nearby provides convenient and step-free access to the large and beautiful walled garden

Steps without handrails can be difficult for many people to use and some people may need a choice of using their left or right hand. This arrangement of a staircase with a single central handrail at Camden Arts Centre is an innovative design solution

The temporary internal ramp at Norton Priory Museum does not disturb the historic fabric

If the cill of an existing doorway can be lowered to eliminate the steps, it may be possible to provide step-free entry into the building. This may appear to be a radical alteration to a historic building, but the benefits are the elimination of any external ramp or lift, if the change of level can be accommodated by an internal lift. A similar arrangement can be adopted by reducing the cill height of an existing window in order to form a new doorway with step-free entry.

When space and resources allow, new step-free entry into a building can be provided by:

■ reducing the cill of an existing doorway (National Gallery)

■ the formation of a new entrance in an existing annex to the existing building (Hollytrees Museum, Captain Cook Museum)

■ a new entrance in the basement or lower ground floor (The Queen's House, Camden Arts Centre)

■ construction of a new extension (Towneley Hall Museum, Sunderland Museum, Dulwich Picture Gallery, Horniman Museum, Norton Priory, the Lighthouse)

© Jonathan Goldberg

Automatic sliding glass doors provide easy access to the new entrance to Hollytrees Museum, where an internal lift serves the upper floors

Locating ancillary activity areas in an annex, basement or extension

If the entrance, reception area and shop in an old building can be located in an annex at the side of, or below, the main building this takes the pressure off the historic spaces. Examples include:

- use of an existing annex (Hollytrees Museum, Captain Cook Museum)

- basement or lower level (The Queen's House, Camden Arts Centre)

- new extension (Dulwich Picture Gallery, Horniman Museum, Towneley Hall Museum, the Lighthouse, Norton Priory, Sunderland Museum)

© Jonathan Goldberg

The new reception area at Sunderland Museum meets most of the design criteria for disabled people so unobtrusively that most people would not notice this – an excellent example of inclusive design

Legible layout: primary circulation routes

In a large and complicated building, the concept of primary access routes can greatly assist in the planning, design and indeed in the use of the building. If the main access routes can be defined and identified easily, the benefits are significant, including reducing the need for elaborate internal signage. This can allow other routes, particularly via historic stairs which may be difficult to adapt, to be left unchanged because the use of these is entirely optional when lift access is available.

A typical example of a feature not changed would be a main staircase which is one of the most important architectural features of a 17th or 18th century house, with marble or timber treads, and often with very limited contrasts of colour and tone. In historic terms, any attempt to add visible nosing strips would be very undesirable and, for people who cannot use stairs, the discreet installation of a lift can provide easier and safer access between floor levels. The Queen's House and Hollytrees Museum are relevant examples.

In a complex building, clear internal routes help people find their way around and reduce the need for internal signage. This is helped by easily identifiable central spaces, such as a courtyard or light-well, and views out to recognisable features.

The following features improve wayfinding, including for those with learning difficulties:

- signage with clearly identifiable symbols and colour coding

- clear circulation and orientation, for example, central spaces, or views out to recognisable features

- central vertical space

- varied visual and tactile information

- active role for disabled people, as in the gardens at Norton Priory

© Jonathan Goldberg

Where adequate alternative routes such as lifts are available and clearly signed, historic staircases like the Tulip stairs at the Queen's House may be left virtually unchanged and used by those who choose to do so

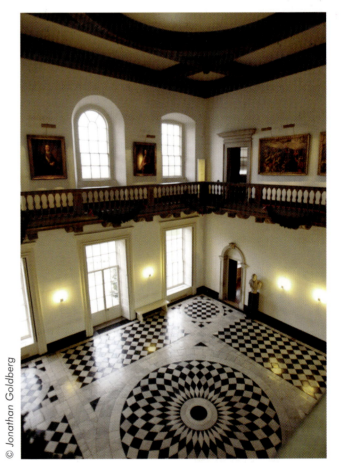

© Jonathan Goldberg

The Great Hall at the Queen's House – an impressive historic and architectural space, can be kept free of clutter because of the new entrance at basement level. Views of the hall help visitors to be aware of their location in the building

The open courtyard at the Fisheries Museum, with a sloping path, is an important feature in this small museum which has very complicated internal circulation routes

Step-free access internally

Changes of level within the buildings were dealt with as follows:

- The Queen's House – by removing a relatively recent staircase to provide space for a new lift and staircase
- National Portrait Gallery – by extending into an under-used space between the National Gallery and the National Portrait Gallery with a new lift and escalator
- Hollytrees Museum – by forming a lift shaft in a later annex, with entry doors concealed in panelling, to provide access to the upper floors of the original building
- Towneley Hall – by providing a platform lift to accommodate a change of level at ground level, plus a passenger lift between the ground and first floors
- Sunderland Museum – with a major new lift and service core
- Fisheries Museum – with a series of internal ramps designed to provide a sequential visit to the exhibition
- Dulwich Picture Gallery – with a new internal ramp to the level of the main gallery
- Horniman Museum – with a major new extension, including a passenger lift and internal ramp
- National Gallery – by inserting an enclosed platform lift inside the new entrance to the original building and with a new lift in a former courtyard
- Camden Arts Centre – by the formation of a lift and staircase in the new extension, with access to the upper floors of the original building
- Norton Priory – with temporary ramps at the main entrance and to the medieval undercroft
- Captain Cook Museum – by inserting a new lift adjacent to the chimney breast of the old domestic building and concealing this within panelling
- Lighthouse – with a major new extension, including a passenger lift
- The Queen's Gallery – by a new lift and staircase within the shell of the reconstructed interior

Access to difficult-to-reach places

It is not always possible to provide physical access to all the interesting parts of an existing building, as this provision could have a negative effect on the historic fabric of the building. Innovative means can be used to provide a comparable visitor experience for those unable to reach these places.

Passenger lifts

The provision of new passenger and platform lifts has been a key element in the improvement of access in many existing museums and art galleries, including the Queen's Gallery, National Portrait Gallery, Hollytrees Museum, Towneley Hall Museum, Sunderland Museum, Horniman Museum, Camden Arts Centre, the Lighthouse and Captain Cook Museum. As the key feature of a primary circulation route, the design of lifts is crucial for independent access by disabled people, especially if the lifts are sufficiently large to be used in company with other people.

Lifts may have to be of the minimum size for wheelchair users (approximately 1100mm by 1400mm), if they are to be inserted into the structure of a historic building with the minimum of structural alterations. They also need to be unobtrusive in sensitive historic environments.

Platform lifts are slow and have been used in very few of the buildings included in this study, mainly because when making alterations to eliminate steps it is often better to provide a ramp or a passenger lift. There are only two, very different examples of platform lifts:

- an open platform lift at Towneley Hall Museum

- a fully enclosed platform lift which operates like a passenger lift at the National Gallery

There is a long climb up the staircase to the tower at the Lighthouse, so this is supplemented by a remotely controlled telescope in order to allow everyone to enjoy the views from a lower level

© Jonathan Goldberg

Captain Cook Museum: in this case the lift is located unobtrusively behind the timber door on the left of the fireplace

Sunderland Museum: a glass lift which provides opportunities for high-level views requires careful design of the floor, guard rails and controls if it is not to cause problems for visually impaired and other disabled people

Easy access to information and exhibits

Choices about the format and content of the information may include:

■ large print, using a font without serifs, such as Helvetica or Arial, both on fixed information panels and on boards or sheets which visitors can take to the exhibits

Tactile map at the entrance to Hollytrees Museum

■ audio descriptions and commentaries available on the internet, CDs or DVDs, and with audio guides. Recent technical developments are making audio guides increasingly easy to use, providing visitors with a choice of exhibits, summaries or detailed information as selected, plus volume control and choice of language. The handsets vary in ease of use, some of the easiest to use being based on the keypad of mobile phones. In contrast, some older systems, with large numbers of buttons on a hand-held wand, can be very confusing, especially for visually impaired people. Some sophisticated systems are triggered by proximity to features of the building or to displays, and can help to guide visitors through the premises

■ modern digital audio guides, similar in design to mobile phones, which give many opportunities for information to be provided in ways to suit the needs of the individual

- tactile information, such as raised maps, models and sculpture, especially when supplemented by audio information, can be very informative and enjoyable for people with impaired vision. The use of Braille is rarely justified, as few people use it, and if located close to a display, there is always the problem of how to find it

- varied visual and tactile displays, with objects to touch, the feel and scent of plants and foliage, and the sounds of water can be informative and enjoyable for all visitors

- language choices for visitors from abroad become practical when audio information is available (although it may not always be cost-effective to do so in Latin!)

- controls to operate information systems, commentaries, displays and lifts to be easy to use and predictable, without making undue demands on manual skills and dexterity

Interpretation and virtual tours

- Models of various kinds are used effectively in many of the museums (The Queen's House, Captain Cook Museum, Hollytrees Museum, Horniman, Norton Priory).

- Maritime models, with excellent illumination and information sheets, and at a height to suit children and wheelchair users, convey a vivid impression of the life and times at Whitby (Captain Cook Museum: model of a sailing ship).

© Jonathan Goldberg

Hollytrees Museum: the layout and design of a museum should enable the arrangements for interpretation and education to develop continuously long after the building works have been completed

- Interactive displays designed to appeal to children and other age groups are used effectively at Sunderland and Hollytrees.

- DVDs and videos can be useful in many ways, including to show spaces which are inaccessible to wheelchair users and other people (Towneley Hall Museum, the Lighthouse, Captain Cook Museum).

Lighting and illumination

Glaring light can be problematic for many people and glare-free illumination is important in order to reduce the problems for visually impaired people. These may include older people who, while not considering themselves to be disabled, can be very sensitive to glare and to abrupt transitions between brightness and darkness.

All the premises included in this study have reasonable transitional illumination to cover the visual change from external conditions, whether from bright sunshine or from twilight on dark, winter evenings. In all cases, the entrance lobby, reception hall and foyer provide space and time for the eye to adapt when entering or leaving the premises (The Queen's House, Hollytrees Museum, Towneley Hall Museum, Dulwich Picture Gallery).

Within historic buildings, traditional illumination, with a combination of natural lighting and a variety of small light sources including chandeliers and candle lamps, use techniques which have been refined over centuries. In some circumstances, traditional lighting may not achieve levels of illumination which are sufficient for modern display requirements, but this can be supplemented by display case lighting or by spotlights concealed behind cornices or other architectural features, or located discreetly in chandeliers and other hanging lamps. New lighting techniques, including fibre-optic installations, give exciting opportunities for improving displays of exhibits and, when necessary, for the conservation of vulnerable materials (Towneley Hall Museum, Captain Cook Museum, Sunderland Museum and Winter Gardens).

Internal courtyards can be very effective for transitional illumination and for providing visitors with awareness of their location and of external weather conditions (Fisheries Museum, Fife).

© Jonathan Goldberg

The natural lighting at Dulwich Picture Gallery, designed by John Soane in the early 19th century, continues to provide excellent conditions, without glare, for looking at pictures

Occasionally, conservation requirements necessitate very low levels of illumination at about 50 lux, and in these situations the transitional lighting needs particular care if people are to be able to see at all on entering the displays of fragile exhibits, for example fabrics, books, watercolours and so on. In some situations, such as at Towneley Hall in 2004, a display of church vestments was not very successful because the exhibits were very difficult to see until the eye had adjusted to the low levels of illumination, only to be followed by the glare from a window directly in front as one entered the chapel.

Acoustics and hearing enhancement

Features that assist include:

■ suitable illumination for lip-reading at the reception desk and elsewhere if appropriate

■ induction loop, or other hearing enhancement systems, at reception desks and in meeting or conference rooms

■ avoiding noisy spaces with reverberation specially in cafés, where the noise levels can be confusing or make conversation difficult

© Eva Zielinska-Millar

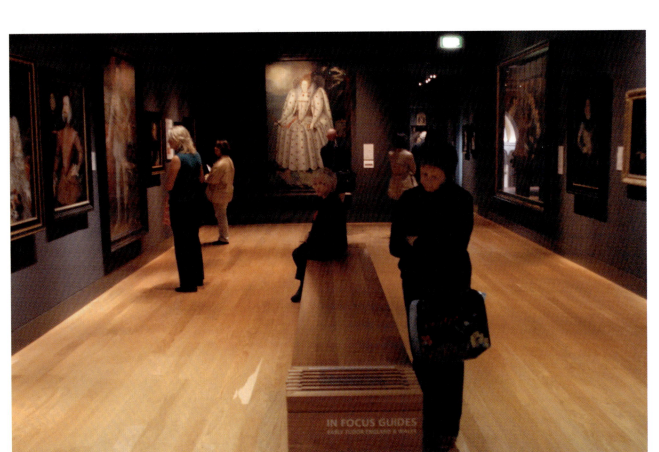

Modern lighting provides opportunities to use a wide range of techniques, from large-scale spaces down to fibre-optics for display cases, for example at the ceiling of the Queen's Gallery (top) and the use of fibre-optics in the Tudor Gallery of the National Portrait Gallery (bottom)

© Jonathan Goldberg

Pressure on numbers at the shop in Hollytrees Museum

Adaptable seating: Towneley Hall Museum

Shops and cafés

A shop is an essential feature for all modern museums and art galleries and an important source of income generation. The location is of paramount importance if the shop is to meet its commercial objectives without causing disturbance within the main exhibition areas.

Ideally, the café should be separated from the main exhibition area in order to minimise disturbance.

The café can be separated in the basement (National Portrait Gallery), at the entrance level (National Gallery, Horniman Museum, Camden Arts Centre), in an extension (Dulwich), or at roof top level (National Portrait Gallery).

Lecture halls and conference rooms

Lecture halls should provide some choice of seating for wheelchair users and people with mobility impairments. There are many advantages in rooms which can be adapted to have level or tiered seating.

WCs

Wheelchair accessible WCs often have white fittings on white walls. These can be difficult to see for visually impaired people and are unnecessarily clinical in appearance.

© Jonathan Goldberg

Dulwich Picture Gallery: a café can be an integral part of a museum, creating a focus for relaxation and refreshment

© Jonathan Goldberg

The use of colour in WCs as at the Queen's House can be both attractive and useful

© Jonathan Goldberg

Sunderland Museum: signage systems should enable visitors to find their way easily within the building and to leave safely in an emergency

Emergency escape

For visitors to make full use of museums and art galleries, they need to be informed about the arrangements and routes for emergency escape. In addition to escape routes being clearly signed and step-free where possible, policies and procedures should be well-coordinated and communicated for the evacuation of disabled people, for safe refuges and for the protection of people with visual or hearing impairments.

Traditionally, fire protection and escape for disabled people were based on independent methods of escape, but more recently, with the recognition that there may be more disabled people at the upper floors of buildings, there is increasing advocacy for systems and procedures for managed escape, including horizontal evacuation and lifts which operate in separate fire zones. Nevertheless, because most people find it natural to leave a building by the way that they came in, the legibility of the layout can be as important for people to leave the premises safely, as it is for them when they arrive.

Historic buildings

The use of a historic building as a museum or an art gallery can be one of the most appropriate ways of ensuring the future viability of the building. The examples of the Queen's House, Hollytrees Museum and Towneley Hall Museum, all show how display and exhibition spaces can be formed without compromising the character of architecturally sensitive spaces.

Accurate historic analysis is essential if access improvements to historic buildings are to be achieved sensitively and successfully. This is important both aesthetically and socially—aesthetically, because important buildings which have been protected and conserved by previous generations are very vulnerable to alterations made for short-term or apparently urgent considerations such as 'compliance' with the DDA. It is also important socially because ill-judged alterations to premises and buildings that people value may provoke the perception that making buildings accessible is more about political correctness than about wider social benefits. A more successful approach is to try to carry out discreet and unobtrusive changes, so that the historic environment becomes inclusively easier for all people to use and enjoy.

Several principles can provide the guidelines for successful access improvements to historic buildings.

Historic analysis can help to identify:

- stages in the development of the building and of later alterations
- significant and less-significant areas of the premises
- original concepts for the buildings if not fully achieved
- areas which offer opportunities for possible access improvements

---

The appraisal of options may include:

- temporary improvements, which are usually reversible
- external improvements, often reversible and usually intrusive (for example ramps, wheelchair platform stairlifts, platform lifts and so on)
- internal improvements, which can often be integrated unobtrusively
- entry via an annex, basement or possibly a new extension
- entry via a reduced threshold level at an existing door or window
- internal vertical circulation, usually via a lift and especially where this can be unobtrusive
- ways to take pressure of visitor numbers off the most sensitive historic areas of the premises
- ways to develop under-used areas to create new commercial opportunities (for instance a shop, a café, meeting rooms and so on)

Many of the most successful access improvements have been achieved by providing step-free entry into the premises, with carefully located internal lifts to provide access to other levels. Even when this involves alterations to the external appearance of a historic building, as at the Queen's House or the National Gallery, the changes can be justified by the ease with which everyone can enter by the same route and reach the other floor levels by internal lifts, avoiding the need for external ramps or platform lifts.

The case studies include examples of historic analyses and of access improvements which illustrate all the examples outlined above. The most successful examples involve bold interventions to achieve inclusive access, but always with a clear and sensitive response to the qualities of the historic fabric.

Conclusions

The main conclusions from this study of 14 museums and art galleries are as follows.

❶ Viable uses for historic buildings

When seeking a viable future for a historic building, one of the best options can be for the building to be used as a museum or an art gallery because the exhibitions and displays can be adapted in response to the history and qualities of the building. A thorough analysis and understanding of the history of the premises is required in order to ensure the alterations achieve a satisfactory balance between conservation and innovation.

(The Queen's House, Hollytrees Museum, Towneley Hall Museum, Norton Priory, Captain Cook Museum)

Captain Cook Museum, view from the gallery: use of a museum or an art gallery can be an effective way of ensuring the future viability of a historic building because the displays can be adapted to suit the characteristics of the building with minimal alterations

❷ Providing step-free entrances to historic buildings

Many historic buildings have steps up to the main entrance. Elegant and step-free access can often be provided via a new entrance at ground level, enabling the character of the original entrance to be unchanged and the changes of level to be dealt with internally, with lifts or ramps.

(The Queen's House, Dulwich Picture Gallery, National Gallery, Camden Arts Centre, Hollytrees Museum, Towneley Hall Museum)

© Jonathan Goldberg

Sunderland Museum: café in the new extension adjacent to the Winter Gardens

❸ Locating ancillary spaces in less sensitive areas

The qualities of a historic building, which is to be used as a museum or an art gallery, can be protected if the ancillary functions (for instance reception, cloakrooms, WCs, shop, café, meeting and conference rooms and so on) are located in an annex or basement, taking the pressure of visitors and facilities away from the more vulnerable parts of the premises. Added benefits are that the ancillary spaces can be used independently, often for income generating activities.

(Dulwich Picture Gallery, National Portrait Gallery, National Gallery, Camden Arts Centre, Hollytrees Museum, Towneley Hall Museum, Norton Priory, Captain Cook Museum, the

Lighthouse, The Queen's Gallery, Fisheries Museum)

❹ Clear principal circulation routes

A fully accessible and legible layout for the principal circulation routes can:

- make the premises easier and more enjoyable for people to visit

- reduce the need for signage

- reduce the need for alterations to secondary routes, such as external steps, internal staircases, doorways and so on

© Jonathan Goldberg

The Queen's House: providing level and step-free entry into an historic building may be less intrusive than the installation of an external ramp or wheelchair lift up to the front door. Internal lifts, or possibly ramps, can then be used unobtrusively for access between internal floor levels

Horniman Museum: fully accessible and clearly marked routes, defined as the primary circulation routes, may make other access issues easier to resolve, and reduce the need for extensive alterations in other parts of the premises

■ ensure that the routes and management arrangements for emergency escape are fully integrated into the layout of the premises

(The Queen's House, Dulwich Picture Gallery, National Portrait Gallery, Camden Arts Centre, Hollytrees Museum, Captain Cook Museum, The Queen's Gallery)

❺ Consultation with users

An inclusive approach to the design and management of the physical, sensory and intellectual features of the premises can provide variety, options and choices to the benefit of all visitors. This process is unlikely to be successful without thorough consultation with user groups.

(Sunderland Museum, The Queen's House, Hollytrees Museum, Towneley Hall Museum, Norton Priory, Captain Cook Museum, the Lighthouse, Fisheries Museum)

Note that disabled people are not referred to in any of these five conclusions because an inclusive approach to design and management can bring benefits to visitors of all ages, abilities, interests, education and nationalities.

The observations and conclusions from this study are set out in more detail in the case studies.

Norton Priory: variety and choice, particularly in access to information and exhibits, can be of great assistance to visitors and increase their enjoyment and response to the displays

View of the Queen's House from across the Thames

The Queen's House, Greenwich

Client:	National Maritime Museum
Architect:	Allies and Morrison
Access Consultant:	David Bonnett Associates
English Heritage:	Paul Calvocoressi

Overview

by Adrian Cave

If a single idea can encapsulate the concept of access with elegance, this is demonstrated at the Queen's House. The classic problem of access into historic buildings is that most have a flight of steps up to the main entrance. The Queen's House, designed by Inigo Jones in 1616 and completed in 1635, was the first Renaissance building in England. This set the pattern for subsequent buildings in the classical style, with a double flight of steps up to the main central door on the north side. The building is symmetrical and provides the axis which formed the basis for Sir Christopher Wren's massive and equally symmetrical composition for Greenwich Hospital (now the Old Royal Naval College), completed in about 1752. The other notable feature of the House is that it was built as two separated blocks on the north and south sides of the former Deptford to Woolwich road (moved north to form the present Romney Road in the 1690s), with the first floor forming a bridge across the old roadway. From this, small doorways, with short steps up immediately inside, were the usual visitor entrances and exits from the time it became a public building in 1937 until 1990.

After less-radical options had been considered, the active support of English Heritage was gained for a bold initiative to provide a new accessible entrance on the northern central axis. This has been the main public frontage of the House and what are now the flanking wings of the National Maritime Museum (NMM) (of which it is part) since about 1860, when railings replaced the walls that used to flank Romney Road between the House and the former Naval College.

This north entrance, down two or three pre-existing outside steps into the basement (ground level on the north side), had become the main public entrance in 1990 as part of a major renovation programme completed at that time. It had already brought significant advantages, allowing the public reception area, cloakrooms and WCs to be located at basement level, leaving the two main floor levels (upper ground floor and first floor) clear and uncluttered for the display, first, of the architecture itself and, second, of the historic pictures of the NMM's important paintings collection. That said, the unobtrusiveness of the basement door itself, without any visual sense of approach, and the steps down to it, still constituted a problem.

Providing full accessibility into the Queen's House via the basement involved the

New step-free entrance at the Queen's House

The uncluttered Great Hall, which provides a central focus to the Museum

Gallery in the Queen's House

installation of a lift into one of the most architecturally sensitive buildings in the country. Research revealed that a secondary internal wooden stairway, in two unmatched sections, had been a relatively late addition and, again with the active support of English Heritage, it was decided to remove this stairway in order to create space for the construction of a new lift and staircase. The only loss of original structure was a small section of the brick vaulting between the basement and the floor immediately above. The need for access through the lift shaft from opposing ends of each floor, however, means that the space for the lift itself is very restricted – effectively a third of the area of the shaft with the stairway occupying another third. The lift car is, therefore, only 1070mm deep and 2070mm wide, more restricted for wheelchair users than the recommended minimum platform size of 1400mm deep by 1100mm wide. However, it was concluded that it would be more reasonable to have a lift with a restricted space than no lift at all. Most people with a manual wheelchair, or with a small electric wheelchair, are now able to visit all the public areas on the three floors of the Queen's House.

This has been achieved without compromising the architectural quality of the building, or the elegant display of pictures and other exhibits in their historic context. Most of the written panels and labels are provided at levels and in formats legible for most people, whether standing or in wheelchairs, and information is also available in other formats when required.

The access improvements at the Queen's House are a notable example of access with elegance at a significant and very sensitive historic building.

Client's account

by Helene Mitchell, National Maritime Museum

'Throughout its history of over 300 years, the Queen's House has been used for its intended purpose for only seven, from 1635–42. Even then, what the House represented to architect and patron was… ephemeral and accessible, physically and conceptually, only to a few.' These assertions by John Bold (in *Greenwich: An Architectural History of the Royal Hospital for Seamen and the Queen's House*) are hard to refute, but with the new millennium came several changes which have opened up the House in every sense.

Brief history of the Queen's House

Inigo Jones designed and began the Queen's House in 1616–17 for Anne, wife of James I, but her death and lack of money delayed its completion until about 1635, when Charles I and his queen, Henrietta Maria, used it as a 'House of Delight' for a few years before the Civil War. A rural retreat set behind the Royal Palace of Greenwich by the river, it was in effect two buildings with a linking first floor 'bridge' which straddled the busy Deptford to Woolwich road. Jones' clever design allowed the court to cross from the Palace gardens to the Park without muddying its feet.

Two further bridge rooms were added in the 1660s, when Charles II required more accommodation, thereby transforming the ground plan of the House from an 'H-shaped' into the square building we see today (see drawings pp 28–29). The 'road' still bisects the

House, but while this affords a marvellous vista along the east/west axis, (see p 33), it also poses major access problems. These are compounded by the difference in north-to-south ground levels – south being nearly 2m higher – and the early 19th century colonnades that connect the House to flanking wings. Built with the colonnades, the wings augmented the House in its late-Georgian conversion as a naval orphanage school, formally renamed the Royal Hospital School in 1892.

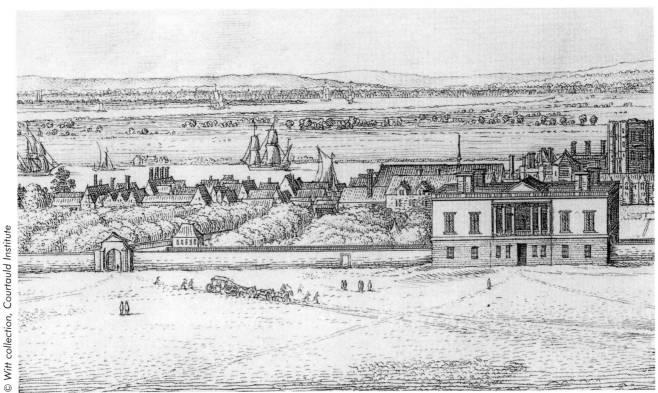

© Witt collection, Courtauld Institute

This detail from Hollar's 1637 Panorama of Greenwich shows the newly completed Queen's House from the park. The wall flanking the Woolwich–Deptford Road is clearly shown, with the Palace of Placentia beside the Thames

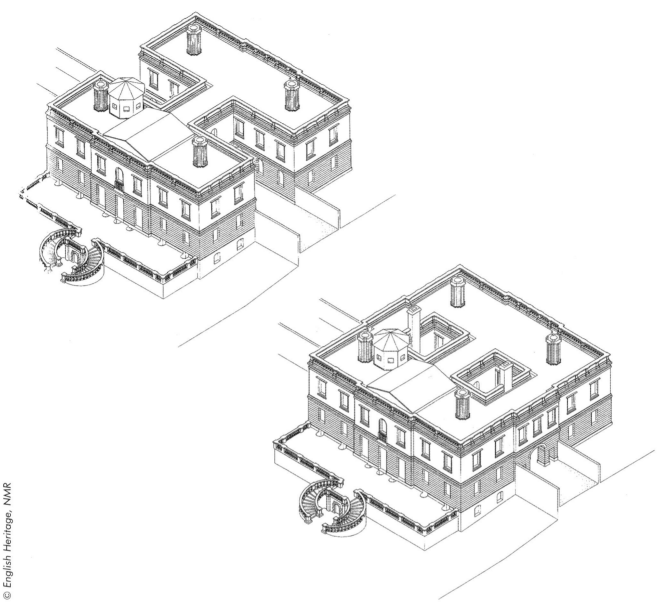

© English Heritage, NMR

The building phases of the Queen's House, based on structural and documentary analysis. The original 'H' becomes a square with the additional bridge rooms, creating a King's side to the east and a Queen's side to the west

National Maritime Museum

When the NMM was established in 1934, it was agreed that it would occupy all these buildings, which the School had just vacated, with the Queen's House as its centrepiece. The Museum has managed the House ever since, using it as a series of galleries to display its collections, especially paintings, although never in ideal conditions. In 1984, a working party led by Richard Ormond (Director of NMM,1986–2000) was set up to reconsider the House's future and the way it was to be presented to the public. £3.5m was spent on major restoration work, with English Heritage closely involved.

The intention was to 'respect and preserve the surviving historic fabric', so perhaps it was not surprising that the reaction of English Heritage and the architectural establishment was totally negative when in 1986 the Museum proposed inserting a lift. There was a precedent for such an 'intrusion': Het Loo (a late 17th century hunting lodge in Holland) had recently undergone major restoration work, including the successful installation of a small lift, but for one of England's earliest and finest classical buildings, this was considered unacceptable. The idea was quickly abandoned and an opportunity lost.

The Queen's House looking east and clearly showing the different ground levels, with the 19th century colonnades and East Wing by Daniel Alexander

Impetus for change

During the 1990s, the Museum increasingly accepted the need for improved access, both physical and intellectual. In 1989, it had created the post of access officer and set up a working group of representatives from across the organisation to keep abreast of changes taking place in accessibility provision. Regular meetings were held, training offered and conferences attended, with modest financial support. The NMM was the first national museum formally to adopt a Disability Access Policy, just a year after the DDA 1995, and it maintained a reputation for being 'ahead of the game' throughout the Act's successive phases. While some disabled people were soon able to appreciate the history and architecture of the Queen's House through the imaginative

use of raised drawings, audio guides and handling materials, it none the less remained completely inaccessible for anyone in a wheelchair. Mobile ramps were tried but deemed too unstable for safety.

In 1997, the Museum decided to hold a major exhibition in the Queen's House to mark the millennium. This required it to revisit the whole issue of how the House should be used. By then it was unthinkable to mount an international exhibition without 'access for all', and the Director set up a small working party to address the challenge. Once again English Heritage was approached: this time, 10 years on, they were prepared to accept the need, but with the proviso that the changes were to be discreet and 'of the highest architectural quality'.

Selecting the architects

Three architects were approached. Stanton Williams, who had very successfully modified the Museum's old Royal Observatory buildings in Greenwich Park for their re-opening in 1993, were eager to be considered. Julian Harrop Architects and Allies and Morrison were also short-listed, since both had extensive experience of working within historic buildings and dealing with English Heritage, Commission for Architecture and the Built Environment (CABE) and other advisory bodies. The complexities of the building were known to all the candidates, but site visits confirmed the problems. The client brief was kept simple: to provide wheelchair access to as much of the Queen's House as possible.

Stanton Williams were the first to submit their proposals in the late summer of 1997. Theirs was a radical approach. The visitor entrance would be via the Orangery, facing the Park, with a lift going up from the basement kitchens through two cabinet rooms on the south side. At ground level, glazed links under the east and west bridge rooms would overcome the problem of the bisecting road. The concept was very bold and not only English Heritage quailed at the prospect: the

Client baulked too! It did, however, prompt the Museum to re-evaluate the visitor route, both to the House and within it.

There was (and is) no easy solution: its various entry levels, its lack of an obvious front door, the unsightly requirements for ticketing and cloakrooms, all had to be considered in the light of accommodating disabled people. The brief was accordingly tightened for the two other contenders. The entrance would be from the north through the door under the terrace, requiring an external ramp down; the basement would provide the necessary visitor facilities and lead to the lift, which, with a stairway, would be accommodated within a space occupied by an existing backstair (see plan below).

Julian Harrop was not convinced that both a lift and stair could be squeezed into this area and he thought it probable that the wall to the first floor Queen's Ante-Room would have to be removed, as well as its fireplace. This was worryingly intrusive, and when Allies and Morrison's feasibility study showed both a generous lift and a refined stair fitting neatly within the allocated space, the Museum had little hesitation in appointing them, with Diane Haigh as project architect, in January 1998.

FIRST FLOOR

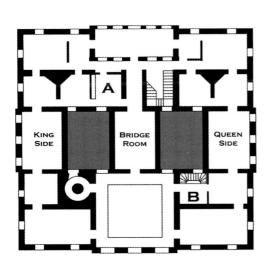

GROUND FLOOR

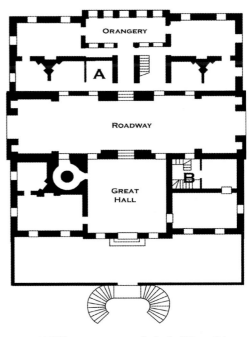

Plan of the Queen's House as restored in 1990. (A) shows where Stanton Williams proposed their lift, with (B) indicating where the lift was installed in 1999

Consultation

This did not leave much time as the millennium exhibition, *The Story of Time*, was scheduled to open on 1 December 1999. Consents and permissions were sought and granted. The Museum of London Archaeological Service was commissioned to undertake the extensive surveys required by English Heritage. John Bold (from the Royal Commission of Historical Monuments of England) and Gordon Higgott (English Heritage) were frequently on site, advising as to what the brickwork revealed, or a fragment of 18th century plasterwork might confirm. The only loss of original fabric was a small section of brick vaulting between basement and ground floor levels.

In July 1998, David Bonnett Architects were appointed to act as the project's architectural access consultants. Apart from his informed advice and technical expertise, the Museum came to appreciate David's sympathetic approach to 'the art of the possible'. He accepted that, very occasionally, best practice and optimum solutions had to be compromised because of the iconic nature of the building, but he also knew when to stand his ground.

The Museum's access officer, Jane Dewey, was involved early in the project to add her experience to the design details. She invited Tony Davis, Greenwich borough access officer, to attend meetings with the architects where he offered useful and practical advice. A contingent of local wheelchair users tested the proposed wheelchair route, which as nearly as possible followed that for the general public, and declared themselves well satisfied. Signage issues were addressed with the advice of a visually impaired consultant and an audio loop was installed.

Regular work-in-progress meetings were held between architects and staff, particularly important for the front-of-house teams and the NMM education department. The latter had ambitious plans for interpretation programmes and events in the House, and early in the project it was decided that two rooms adjacent to the lift and near the entrance would be allocated for their use. Care was taken to equip and furnish these rooms with easy access in mind. In short, there was a concerted attempt to inform the architects of access needs as perceived by the client.

Successful conclusion

In May 2001, the Museum re-launched the House as a showcase for its extensive and valuable art collection. A discreetly flexible lighting system ensures that paintings can be properly viewed and the building's classical architecture fully appreciated. Apart from the difficulty of crossing the bisecting road at ground level, everyone can now reach every part of the building and enjoy its interiors. As with many good solutions, several benefits have resulted from the changes. The lift not only accommodates two wheelchair users at a time but also allows for the convenient movement of large and heavy artefacts. The new stairs are not only aesthetically an improvement on the indifferent 19th century wooden ones they replace; they are also safer and provide a continuous link to all three floors on the west side of the Great Hall, which was not previously the case.

The gently inclining stone path leading to the basement door on the northern central axis now attractively defines the approach to the entrance, at the original 17th century ground level, serving both the general public and the wheelchair user alike. The basement has been re-rendered to create a more easily navigable area for visitors and leads conveniently both to the lift and the improved, accessible cloakroom. On the south (Greenwich Park) side of the House, a concealed Portland stone ramp was included in the project, obviating the need to negotiate the low steps into the Orangery, a space frequently used for events and corporate entertainment (see photo below).

The Museum regards this as an extremely successful project. The alterations have been elegantly achieved at a cost of less than

Ramp improving access to the south front

£1million and within tight time constraints, and English Heritage have rightly declared them 'exemplary'.

Architect's account

by Diane Haigh, Allies and Morrison

The Queen's House was designed by Inigo Jones to span between two worlds: between the safe walled enclosure of the riverside Tudor palace of Placentia and the 'wilderness' of the hunting park beyond. In making this leap, it bridged over the main riverside road into London. This has meant that circulation in the house was inherently complex, as the first floor apartments had always been the only level to link across the road.

The Queen's House was unsuitable for use as a gallery without inclusive access. Keen to stage their millennium exhibition *The Story of Time* there, the clients commissioned Allies and Morrison to explore ways of making the Queen's House fully accessible which might also be permitted by English Heritage in this most sensitive Ancient Monument.

Full inclusive access required:

■ a new visitor entrance which would not involve stairs

■ installation of a lift to serve all levels

■ fully accessible toilet provision

These features were to be an integrated part of the circulation pattern for all visitors. Previously, the visitor entrance to the Queen's House had been through small side doors from the former central carriageway into,

respectively, the Great Hall on the north side and a corridor on the south, both of which involved negotiating two sets of steps from the colonnades. Attention turned to achieving level access through the central basement door, placed axially on the north front, down a short flight of steps.

The external ground level was lowered by a new, gently dished, semi-circular forecourt forming a shallow ramp down to this doorway. The axis of the building is emphasised by a tongue of paving leading directly down to the original entrance door. Inigo Jones' original door surround is still to be found on an inner wall. This now provides a clear and accessible entrance for all visitors from where the gallery tour starts.

The location of the new lift and stair was the next issue to be addressed, to take visitors from the basement to the two upper gallery floors. Symmetrically opposite the original Tulip Stairs across the Great Hall was a space containing a contorted staircase, a much later addition. As the brick vault to the basement had already been broken through here to take a staircase in 1989, this seemed to be the one place where a lift shaft could be inserted without loss of intact fabric.

The new staircase was designed as a cantilever stair on the same structural principle as the

The view from east to west showing the underside of the bridge rooms crossing what is now a cobbled courtyard

Inigo Jones' sketch for the Queen's House

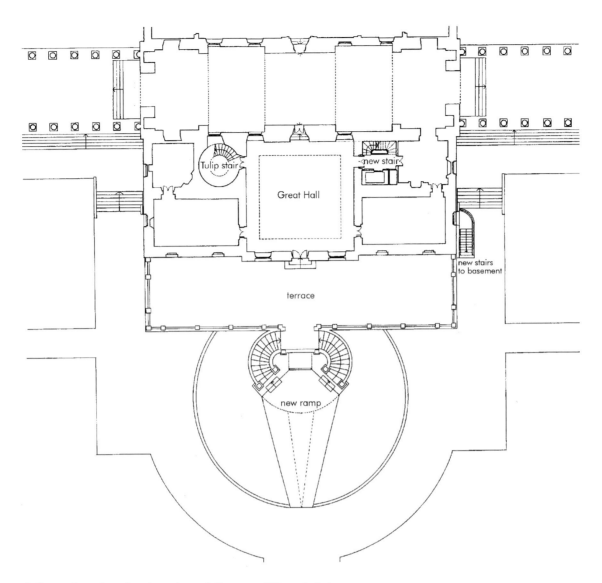

Ground floor plan showing location of the new lift and stairs

Tulip Stairs. Treads are made of pre-cast concrete units, the load being transferred vertically from tread to tread. A steel string bolted to the face of the brick shaft takes the torsion load and locates the risers. A continuous bronze handrail follows the sinuous curve of the new three-storey staircase. The balustrade is made of steel strips woven into a grid, which distorts around the circular riser sections – a visual parallel to the geometric patterns of the black-and-white paving in the Hall which transform from square to circle. Visitor circulation has been transformed by this second stair, which now allows a circuit through the galleries with one route up and the other down.

Within the basement, the brick vaults have been re-rendered with a rough lime render. The original 1617 brickwork had been exposed in the 1989 restoration work carried out by the Property Services Agency of the Department of the Environment. A Victorian cementitious render had been removed and the badly spalled brickwork had been repaired in places and left exposed. After much debate, it was agreed that originally the brickwork had been intended to be rendered, as it contained so many original inconsistencies in vaulting, many cut bricks and uneven coursing. Keying scratches in the brickwork revealed the presence of an early lime mortar. It was replaced with a traditional lime render so that the space is now lighter and clearer, as it would have been when additional north windows were closed by the addition of the north terrace in the 1630s. The rough finish of the render follows the uneven surface of the brickwork below like a stretched skin and in places reveals the bricks below.

This project has given the Queen's House complete museum visitor facilities for the first time. Now, the information desk,

© Jonathan Goldberg

New stair using the same restricted but now well used vertical space as the lift

© Jonathan Goldberg

Inigo Jones' Tulip stairs remain unchanged

cloakroom, shop and toilets are discreetly located in the basement. They mark the start and finish of a coherent visitor route through the house, which step by step reveals the significance of this milestone in British architectural history.

English Heritage's account

by Paul Calvocoressi, former Inspector of Historic Buildings, English Heritage

Considerations for access in historic buildings

The Queen's House at Greenwich is one of the first true Renaissance buildings in England and, as such, a major landmark in our architectural history. It is a scheduled ancient monument, a Grade I listed building, and a centrepiece of the Maritime Greenwich World Heritage site.

Since 1937, it has been open to the public as part of the NMM.

Because of its status as a scheduled monument, scheduled monument consent from the Secretary of State for Culture, Media and Sport was required for the access improvement works that are the subject of this study. English Heritage's role was to advise the Secretary of State of the extent to which the monument's special architectural or historic interest would be affected, and to recommend whether or not consent should be granted.

The Queen's House

It was Queen Anne of Denmark, wife of King James I, who originally commissioned Inigo Jones to build a villa at Greenwich. It was located astride the Greenwich to Woolwich Road, providing access from Greenwich Palace to the park. Work started in 1616, but ceased in 1618 when construction had only reached ground floor level, owing to the Queen's ill-health (she died in 1619). It was taken up again for Charles I's wife, Henrietta Maria between 1620 and 1640, at which time the terrace was added on the north side. After the Restoration in 1660, John Webb, Jones' former assistant, carried on the work, converting Jones' original H-plan villa to its present four-square arrangement by adding the two outer bridges on the first floor. Further alterations were carried out in the 18th century, including changes to the stairs down from the north terrace to accommodate a raised ground floor level; between 1807–16, when the ranges now occupied by the NMM were added; and in the 1930s, when the school, for which these ranges had originally been intended, moved out and the Museum took its place. These works included a major restoration of the Queen's House and there was a further restoration campaign in the late 1980s.

The project

One consequence of this rich and complicated building history was that the horizontal and vertical circulation within the building was both tortuous and difficult, and there was no level access into the building. For a major public museum, this was clearly unsatisfactory. The issue for English Heritage in considering the Museum's proposals to deal with the situation was to ensure that essential access improvements were achieved without compromising the House's integrity as a historic monument, bearing in mind also that for a large proportion of visitors, the house itself was at least as important as the objects being displayed.

The first proposals

English Heritage was first approached by the Museum in 1997 with ideas for improving the internal circulation. These had been prepared by the architects Stanton Williams and included:

- incorporating the roadway space through the building by enclosing it

- improving circulation and means of escape at ground floor level by forming new doorways into the road, and

- the provision of a lift to serve all three floors

These ideas were considered by English Heritage's London Advisory Committee in October 1997 after a site visit, and it was felt that the first two would both seriously harm the historic relationship of the house to its site. However, the possibility of introducing a lift did seem worth pursuing, although it was felt that the Backstairs compartment on the north side of the building, west of the Great Hall, and behind the Queen's Bedchamber, would be a less disruptive location than the site on the south side of the roadway originally suggested.

Development of proposals

The Museum then decided to abandon the two proposals affecting the roadway, and in 1998, the architects, Allies and Morrison, were appointed to work up ways of improving access. Their proposals included a new staircase and lift internally, and ramped access from the exterior.

The lift and staircase

The Backstairs compartment was agreed to be the only appropriate location. At the time, it was occupied by three separate stairs, of which the ground floor to basement flight was part of the 1990s re-ordering, and the flights between the ground floor and mezzanine and the mezzanine and first floor were relatively modest examples dating from the earlier 19th century. It was clear from earlier plans that the space had been intended from the start for vertical circulation (balancing the Tulip Stair on the other side of the Great Hall), but the existing fabric was mostly of much more recent date.

The lift shaft was located on the north side of the compartment, making use of the opening cut through the 17th century brick vault for the 1990s basement stair. The staircase ran through the basement to the first floor on the opposite side. The construction also required the loss of the two 19th century stairs and more of the brick vaulting. It was considered, though, that in the circumstances, this was acceptable and that the proposals represented an elegant solution to the problem of providing better access within the house. Moreover, the design of the new stair, with the ingenious balustrading of interwoven metal strips, seems to successfully complement Inigo Jones's Tulip Stair without trying to upstage it.

The ramp

Improvement of the external access presented greater problems. On the south side, access at ground floor level into the Orangery was easy to achieve with the provision of a small, unobtrusive ramp.

However, on the north side, it was not so simple. The existing access was through the central doorway beneath the terrace and, via the narrow basement passage, the original entrance to the basement of 1616–18, involving the descent of four steps into a narrow well in front of the outer threshold (see photo below).

Initially, this seemed to present the most obvious route, but it was felt by the architects that to introduce a ramp to accommodate such a change of level would be architecturally disruptive, particularly to the stairs down from the terrace. The alternative option was to bring the ramp down at the northwest corner of the house, making use of the north window opening on the west side of the basement. This would have advantages in circulation terms, being closer to the lift and to the

Stairs to the north terrace, showing their 18th century form, with the footings to the original 1630s stairs revealed by excavation, September 1999

display areas, but it would also have introduced an eye-catching, asymmetrical element into a strongly symmetrical building, which is part of a powerfully axial overall composition, and it was on this ground that English Heritage raised concerns when the scheme was put to them in July 1998.

This prompted Allies and Morrison to look again at the central axis, and to produce the designs for what was eventually approved and built. The sacrifice required to make the ramp work was the cutting out of the footings to the bottom of the original 1630s stairs, which had survived below ground from when the stairs had been adapted in the 18th century and their replacement, after detailed archaeological recording, with three new steps on each side down to the new level. These are of Portland stone, but detailed in a simpler style, which is clearly of its own date and reads clearly as a late 20th century edition.

Well in front of the north entrance to the basement, before the works, June 1988

Stairs to the north terrace, showing the new steps under construction, October 1998

Balcony Gallery at the National Portrait Gallery

National Portrait Gallery, London

Client:	National Portrait Gallery
Architect:	Dixon Jones

Overview

by Adrian Cave

The idea of 'the deal' which transformed the National Portrait Gallery from a cramped 19th century building to a spacious, modern art gallery overthrew the constraints of the client's original brief. This is an important example of how the ability to think creatively in three dimensions can often be the key to improving access in historic buildings. In this case, the idea was to realise that by an exchange of spaces between the National Portrait Gallery and the National Gallery, there could be unexpected benefits to both.

For the National Portrait Gallery, the most significant advantage of the exchange was the opportunity to create a large central space, brightly lit with natural illumination from above, which could become the main circulation and organisational space of the Gallery, unifying the internal spaces and providing a clear sense of location and orientation for visitors.

A big idea for a historic building is only valid if carried through into the design of spaces, construction and detailing, and this has been achieved at the National Portrait Gallery with consistency and flair. Although the main stepped entrance is almost unchanged, an improved, level entrance nearby provides access into the building and via a platform lift, to the shop and to a new lift which serves all

the main floor levels, including the café in the basement and the restaurant at roof level. The new lift, with doors on three sides to serve intermediate levels, is located adjacent to the main central space providing similar spatial experiences for all visitors to the Gallery, whether they travel by lift, steps or escalator.

Access to the original galleries, which date from the 19th century or early 20th century, is improved in the redevelopment of the spaces and by the new lift, but the real transformation of the Gallery is a result of the dramatic new space containing an escalator and staircase, and by two adjoining new galleries at upper floor levels.

The lower of these two galleries is bright and open to the central space, while the upper gallery is dark and enclosed, with very subdued lighting for the conservation and display of delicate works of art. The two galleries, both with modern features and illumination, are a perfect foil to the earlier and more traditional galleries in the building.

Any visitor to the National Portrait Gallery is led naturally towards the bright space at the heart of the building, with the diagonal lines of the escalator and the staircase leading further upwards. On arriving into this central space, the elegance of the detailing is evident in the materials, handrails and wall lights of the staircase and in the quality of the reception desk. This unobtrusively provides shelves at convenient heights for people who cannot bend down and for those who cannot reach up, and provides this by a simple extension of the staff work surface to one side of the desk, an example of inclusive design with elegance.

The café below pavement level makes ingenious use of the formerly restricted spaces in the basement, while the restaurant at roof level provides extensive views towards Whitehall over Trafalgar Square, which was pedestrianised some five years after the improvements to the National Portrait Gallery. In common with many restaurants of the 1980s and 1990s, the hard surfaces of the restaurant cause reverberation and noise levels which make conversation difficult for everyone, and almost impossible for hearing impaired people.

The recent major projects at the National Portrait Gallery and at Trafalgar Square, and the earlier construction of the Sainsbury Wing at the National Gallery, have brought new and very popular activities, cultural uses and aesthetic qualities to this important space in London.

Client's account

John Wykeham, Head of Administration, National Portrait Gallery

Introduction

The National Portrait Gallery, designed by Ewan Christian, first opened its doors on St Martin's Place in 1896. The impression of a cultural fortress created by the moats and sturdy railings that surround the building may not have been dispelled by the interior. The grand, rather processional front staircase led visitors to the upper floors where most of the paintings were hung. For much of the last century, the building was largely unaltered apart from the addition of a new wing in the 1930s and occasional refurbishment in period style. With the increasing popularity of the Gallery's contemporary portraits, programmes of special exhibitions and educational activities, the need to provide more display space and a more modern aspect became pressing.

Development of the ground floor for 20th century displays and special exhibitions, and the creation of an education centre in the 1990s, marked a significant step forward.

Opening up the ground floor and creating a new entrance in Orange Street provided step-free public access to most of the building and underlined the contemporary relevance of the Gallery's work. In doing so, however, the new development also served to increase the sense of focus on the immediately accessible, leaving the period collections on the upper floors more remote than before. Visitor numbers increased from a plateau of circa 600,000 to nearly 900,000, but perhaps only 20 per cent were making their way to these important parts of the displays. The increased popularity of the Gallery also put pressure on us to further improve visitor facilities, particularly a more modern and accessible lecture theatre, visitor information services and somewhere for visitors to enjoy a coffee or lunch. A radical solution, but one that worked in harmony with the historic building, was needed.

In 1994, the Gallery commissioned Jeremy Dixon and Edward Jones to design a new wing, or more accurately a new core to the building. The challenge had been to identify a way in which we could optimise the use of a rear yard sandwiched between our building and the National Gallery, over which our neighbours had rights of light and access. Dixon Jones came up with a proposal that persuaded the National Gallery that they could make effective use of our east wing and that we should offer this in exchange for unfettered development of the yard. The 'deal' was done, and as a result we have effectively been able to create a new building that sits alongside and opens up the 19th century building.

While the new Ondaatje Wing provides a stunningly fresh aspect to the Gallery and modern facilities – a lecture theatre, information centre, IT gallery and restaurant – as well as new display spaces for the Tudor and late 20th century collections, the way in which it allows visitors to understand and to move around the whole site is equally important. Improving physical access was a key requirement of the architects' brief and working within the constraints of the surrounding Grade I listed building was a major challenge. Connecting the new to the old presented some sensitive design issues.

The front entrance and staircase

While the Orange Street entrance had provided easier access into the Gallery, the route to the new ground floor hall from the St

Ground floor plan

The basement café

Martin's Place entrance was barred to visitors with mobility difficulties by Ewan Christian's front entrance steps and imposing staircase.

The front entrance steps posed particular problems, and although ideas were explored at the time, and in a more recent access survey, for various ramps and new openings, they would all involve a significant intervention in the appearance of the main entrance. To circumvent the steps, we introduced a new lift at our nearby shop entrance that both provides level access to the interior and that also helped us to develop the basement beneath as a bookshop and café. This was the one occasion that we felt that it would be unjustified to interfere with an important part of the historic architecture, given that we had a reasonable alternative solution.

Dealing with the staircase proved easier. At the ground floor we created a new connection to an existing lift in a narrow gap that runs alongside the staircase. This gave lift access

from the foyer to the new entrance hall and to the first floor, but not to the second floor galleries where there was yet another change in level between the staircase landing onto which the lift opened and the main floor. The solution was to raise the height of the landing level with the main floor. This meant extending the York stone stairs and creating a new landing with mosaics to match the original – a significant alteration to Ewan Christian's staircase but one that with careful detailing earned the support of English Heritage.

The new entrance hall and vertical circulation core

Making the front lift and staircase work more effectively was important, but it was only a small part of making the building more accessible. The new entrance hall with its escalator that rises directly to second floor galleries and the start of the chronologically ordered displays, the new, first floor balcony

Entrance hall and escalator

the new hall, the only location for lifts seemed to be the rear staircase that had been introduced when the 1930s extension was built. The demolition of this staircase to form a new circulation core with two public lifts and a new stairs might well have brought a veto from English Heritage, but as with the front stairs, we found them sympathetic and supportive of our aims.

New galleries and visitor facilities

If better access was a key driving force behind the scheme, there were of course other equally important objectives. The solutions to our needs now seem beautifully simple and obvious.

The rooftop with its superb views across Whitehall provided the obvious location for a restaurant. Extensively used by our visitors, it has also become a destination restaurant bringing new people to the Gallery and a much-needed source of additional income.

On the second floor of the new wing, at the head of the escalator, we were able to create a display space for the earliest portraits in our collection – key images from the Plantagenet and Tudor periods that had previously languished on one of the landings of the front staircase and were inaccessible by lift.

gallery that opens onto the hall and the large openings into the Ewan Christian building combine to give the building a legibility that was entirely lacking before. It has been described as a referential space and a visual indicator that achieves more than any amount of signage can hope to do.

At the heart of the new hall is an information desk where visitors can plan their visit, obtain a sound guide, or purchase tickets to special exhibitions. On an adjacent mezzanine, visible from the hall, is an IT gallery where visitors can use touch screens to access information and images of all the portraits in the Gallery's collection.

With increasing numbers of visitors anticipated, and the quite understandable demands for easier physical circulation, it was essential that we were also able to introduce more lifts into the building. Without sacrificing the escalator and destroying the character of

View from the rooftop café towards Westminster

On the floor below, a new balcony gallery provided space for the ever-growing collection of 20th century portraits freeing space on the ground floor for contemporary acquisitions.

With education as one of the Gallery's central purposes, we needed a new lecture theatre to replace the antiquated 70-seat room located in one corner of the 19th century display. Situated below the new entrance hall and accessible from the front foyer, the new 150-seat Ondaatje lecture-theatre has proved of huge benefit in developing our programme of lectures, conferences and other activities.

The future

If the Dixon Jones scheme represented another very big step forward in making the National Portrait Gallery a more accessible and enjoyable place to visit, it is by no means the end of the story. Nor does it represent a perfect or complete design solution in terms of making the building fully accessible.

After four years of seeing how our visitors use the building, we have recently commissioned an access audit to look at what further improvements and adjustments can be made. Best practice in design has moved on and we have had time to see what does not work as well as it should. As a result, better accessible toilets, external lighting, clearer signage, doors that are easier to negotiate, a lecture theatre auditorium that can be used more fully by visitors in wheelchairs, are all on our action list along with a number of other small improvements. Perhaps the most important improvement we can make is to provide lift access to the one landing on the front staircase where we still display paintings – the solution adopted to circumvent the first flight of stairs is one that will work here too.

Removing physical barriers, the main focus of this piece, is of course only one component of making the collections accessible and enjoyable for all our visitors. Since 2000, the Gallery has employed a full-time access officer dedicated to improving intellectual access. In consultation with disabled visitors and Gallery staff, the Gallery has developed alternative methods of interpreting the displays to ensure they are accessible to all visitors. The recent refurbishment of galleries displaying portraits from the Regency period has enabled the Gallery to develop highly innovative ways to interpret the collection, introducing IT to the display spaces, tactile information for partially sighted and blind visitors, and additional material on the gallery's sound guide. The use of large print descriptions of paintings and tactile drawings has also been introduced in the Tudor and early 20th century displays. Gallery tours, talks and practical workshops have been established for children and adults with learning difficulties, visually impaired and deaf visitors. These programmes are advertised on the Gallery's website and through publications such as the Royal National Institute of the Blind's (RNIB) *New Beacon* magazine, the Royal National Institute of Deaf People's (RNID) *Sign Matters* journal and websites for BSL users. The Gallery has also published an access leaflet for visitors.

Training Gallery staff in access issues has been of key importance in improving the service we offer visitors. Our access officer provides general disability awareness training for all staff. We also provide more specific training in the areas of mental health, adults with additional needs, visually impaired, hearing impaired and deaf groups. The Gallery has recently piloted a basic British Sign Language course with a deaf consultant that will become part of the Gallery's annual training programme.

In April 2004 the Gallery was awarded the National Excellence in England Gold Award, Tourism for All, for its services and facilities for disabled visitors.

Architect's account

Interview with Edward Jones by Flora Gathorne-Hardy

Q *From your perspective as an architect, how have attitudes towards issues of access and inclusive design changed over recent years?*

A There is a new sensibility towards access. Allowing everyone access to buildings has become second nature. Rather than bolting on changes or relying on codes of conduct you look up in a book, it tends now to come in more automatically. A change of level rings alarm bells.

The student trained in the 1950s or 1960s was not so aware of these issues. There was no vocal lobby. So my generation of architects needed a reassessment, which was not too much of a problem as modernism had always enjoyed ideas of ramps, of looking at the ground as the principal level. The Penguin Pool at London Zoo; Le Corbusier's ramps: these are the icons of modern architecture. On the other hand, the 19th century architect who enjoyed the temple on a plinth, its steps and symmetrical fronts, would have found it much more awkward.

Q *You mention 19th century architectural styles. What problems and opportunities have you encountered in making changes to historical buildings like the National Portrait Gallery?*

A I think a balance is needed – a balance must be sought. If, for example, we reject external flights of stairs, then we write off a great deal of the past and some great moments in architecture. It is interesting that in America in the 19th and early 20th centuries, the plinth and broad flight of stairs appeared on all great public institutions. This big flight of steps on

libraries or city halls represented the breadth of the constituency who were welcome. All could enter. It was a symbol of democracy. Now, you would not do it.

Entrance areas are fundamental. As an architect, you do not want to upset people at the entrance to a building. In our designs we hope to establish the idea that the lift has a place at the entrance as much as the staircase. The vertical and the diagonal are set side by side. In fact, many people do not want to climb the flight of stairs. These are some of the things we think about as we look at different ideas.

But you cannot generalise about how to strike this balance between respecting the integrity of an historic building and improving access. It depends on if the design is any good! I am a believer in applying common sense. Campaigning bodies are important in changing points of view, but there is a danger of polarising arguments and this can create a minefield of problems for the designer.

Spotlights help to make these existing steps visible without physical alterations

Q *You have talked about physical access. Were there other aspects of design that helped make the National Portrait Gallery more inclusive?*

A We thought about lighting. We looked at landings and the edges of stairs. We decided to distinguish the first and bottom tread on the stairs and assume that the motor action of each tread and good lighting would guide people down the flight of stairs. We did not want things to look overly caring. We did not want to be condescending.

We have tackled the questions of information and signage exhaustively for the Royal Opera House and even then confusion can still arise. For the National Portrait Gallery we knew we could rely a great deal upon staff being there to welcome people and answer their questions. I think this is a good solution. A clear plan does not require a lot of signage.

Q *What kind of post-occupancy evaluations do you carry out on projects such as the National Portrait Gallery?*

A Where there is a good rapport with the client as in the case of the National Portrait Gallery, we were very receptive to post-occupancy practical discussions. For example, the Portrait Gallery with its extraordinary view down Whitehall is found to be very noisy for some people. And so as part of our post-occupancy evaluation we are presently reviewing the acoustics. I believe it would be very odd if the architect was not sensitive to issues arising from the building in use.

The new balcony gallery providing space for 20th century portraits, which frees space on the ground floor for contemporary aquisitions

Hollytrees from the north, view from Castle Park, 1999 – before alterations

Hollytrees Museum, Colchester

Client:	Colchester Museums
Architects:	Purcell Miller Tritton
Access Consultants:	Earnscliffe Davies Associates
English Heritage:	Andrew Derrick

Overview

by Adrian Cave

Consultation

Consultation with disabled people was a key factor in the successful improvement programme for this museum, resulting in design and management changes which have contributed to the accessibility and enjoyment of the exhibits by all visitors. The design changes are experienced even before the visitor arrives at the doors of the museum, where a proposed path of deep gravel was changed to a surface of rolled gravel on a firm asphalt base. This is an example of visual design intended to be in harmony with the character of the 18th century building being modified to suit the access needs of everyone. The firm gravel surface is more suitable than soft gravel for wheelchair users, families with children in pushchairs, young children and anyone with mobility impairments, including people who use sticks or crutches.

New entry

Hollytrees Museum is also a useful example of an 18th century building with steps up to the main entrance doors, where a new entrance at the side has provided significant advantages. If the main entry had been maintained at the front door, it would have been necessary to make changes, probably with an external platform lift at the front steps, and even then the front door would have been difficult to open and the entrance hall would have offered only restricted space for the reception area and a shop. The new entrance doors into the side wing are glass and slide open automatically, leading directly into the reception area and the shop, all at ground level and below the level of the original main entrance. The result is that the members of staff are able to run the entrance and shop area without the constraints of a historic interior and to leave the original entrance hall uncluttered for all to see.

The lift

When a lift is required in a historic building to provide access to various floor levels, it is usually most satisfactory if the new lift can be located inside the building in a shaft which can be concealed without alterations to the visible part of the historic fabric. At Hollytrees Museum, this has been achieved by locating the lift shaft in an area of the 18th century extension, with the lift doors on alternate sides

View of Hollytrees from the north – the original house and its 18th century extension

New entrance through arcade in the west wing to the side of the main house

to serve intermediate floor levels. This enables anyone arriving at the level entrance of the reception area to use the lift to reach all the main floor levels. Difficulties in reaching the lift door, due to the lack of a 300mm space at the leading edge of the door, have been imaginatively overcome with a tassel cord on the door handle. This feature, which at first sight appears to be merely eccentric, is in fact an unusual, witty and very practical innovation!

Orientation

Hollytrees Museum is well signed from the entrance to the park in which it is located, with a clear route to the new glass entrance doors. Once inside the building, the main staircase and hallway of the original building provide a clear sense of space and location at all floor levels. For those using the lift, the sense of orientation may be less clear, but in this small building there is little cause for confusion. Tactile plans with good colour contrasts on each floor, produced as a result of a consultation with visually impaired people,

© Jonathan Goldberg

Use of a tassel to open the lift door

are useful for everyone who wishes to find their way around the building.

Displays

The museum is located in a park which also contains the large and impressive structure of Colchester Castle, so the historic context for the museum is evident before one arrives at the museum. With particular emphasis on the educational role of the Museum, the display techniques at Hollytrees Museum include:

- a room furnished to show how it might have been used in the past
- recording of an 18th century description of contemporary life in Colchester
- 18th and 19th century domestic tools and equipment available both to see and to touch
- objects shown with 'shop window' techniques and at low levels to be easy for everyone to see
- a small cupboard with doors which can be opened to reveal objects which can be handled and with an explanation for each. Some of the doors are too high for small children or for wheelchair users, and this was a point which had not been picked up at the design stage
- education rooms, complete with traditional clothes and fancy dress, to assist in role playing while listening to stories about the building and life in the area

Hollytrees Museum has been very successful in attracting local people, and in its educational programme, and has done this in ways which have enhanced rather than compromised the historic quality of this important building.

Client's account

by Tom Hodgson, Curator of Social History, Colchester Museums

Hollytrees is a Grade I listed Georgian town house situated in the centre of Colchester. It sits next to Colchester Castle within Castle Park, a Grade II historic park and in part a scheduled Ancient Monument. It has been described in Pevsner's guide to the buildings of Essex as the best 18th century house in the town.

The house was built in brick in 1718 by a London builder, Thomas Blagden, for Elizabeth Cornelisen, and replaced an earlier property on the site. It was Palladian in design, of three storeys and a basement, and square in plan with a central staircase projecting from the west elevation. Hollytrees passed to the local MP and antiquarian, Charles Gray, in 1727. He added an extension to the west in 1748, designed by James Deane, a local architect (see drawing). This extension allowed the construction of a servants' staircase to the north of the existing staircase, and closets were installed to the northern end of the gap between the west wing and the main house.

After Gray's death in 1782, Hollytrees passed to the Round family, prominent local landowners, and remained in their possession until they sold the house and grounds (now the upper section of the Castle Park) to Colchester Corporation in two stages in 1892 and 1920. Hollytrees was converted into a museum of local mediaeval antiquities and bygones, and opened to the public in 1929. During the museum conversion, the servants' staircase and closets were removed, and an extra floor inserted to accommodate two lavatories and a top floor bathroom for the museum curator who lived 'over the shop'.

Proposal for the west extension by James Deane, 1748

The need for redevelopment of Hollytrees Museum had been recognised for a number of years. There were two driving forces. First, the displays had remained essentially unaltered since the 1970s, and the effect of this was seen in a steady decline in visitor numbers from 28,108 in 1984/1985 to 13,743 in 1998/1999. The museum was clearly failing to provide an acceptable public service to the people of Colchester and to visitors to the town.

Second, Hollytrees was the least physically accessible of the museums in the service as it was approached by steps on all sides and has a complex arrangement of floor levels. The requirements of the DDA, which had recently come into force, and the commitment of Colchester Museums and Colchester Borough Council to increased access made the improvement of access to and within Hollytrees Museum a major and integral element of any redevelopment.

It was vital for the museum service that Hollytrees had a continuing useful life. The key word in discussions with English Heritage over listed building consent was viability. It was considered that as a public building, the only viable future for it was as a museum. Any other function would have created much greater pressures for alteration of the fabric.

An extensive access audit of Hollytrees Museum, commissioned in November 1995 from Earnscliffe Davies Associates, highlighted the problems of access to the building. The recommendations from this report, covering the museum displays as well as the building, informed all subsequent development work.

The architects, Purcell Miller Tritton, were commissioned to carry out a feasibility study on how to redevelop the building. They were chosen for their experience of working with historic buildings and because of their involvement with the museum service on previous work.

The main task was to investigate possible locations for a lift. The access audit had recommended that ideally a lift should be provided, but acknowledged that this would be difficult to achieve given the Grade I listed status. Discussions with English Heritage ruled out an external lift shaft, but the option of a lift between the original block and the 1748 extension was entertained. Detailed research into the building sequence, including an archaeological investigation, showed that this

Pencil drawing of Hollytrees from the north, about 1850

area had been substantially altered in the 1920s.

It soon became clear from the building layout that a lift in the proposed position would require a relocation of the museum entrance if those requiring level or ramped access were not to be segregated from other visitors. This problem was resolved thanks to the documentary research, which revealed that a space being used as a kitchen at the back of the building had originally been an open arcade.

By re-opening the arcade and a blocked doorway in the original building, a circulation route could be created. There were other benefits to having the museum entrance in the Castle Park. A survey had shown that as many people passed Hollytrees on the Castle Park side as on the High Street side. The proposed entrance was easier to reach from Colchester Castle and positioned Hollytrees firmly within the orbit of the leisure activities in the Castle Park. The case for the alterations was accepted by English Heritage and listed building consent was granted in April 1999.

A display brief had been drawn up, and in July 1997, following a standard selection process, Brennan and Whalley were chosen to work up design proposals for a Lottery application in conjunction with Colchester Museums. Earnscliffe Davies Associates gave the proposals an access appraisal in August 1998. This generated positive comment, particularly over the plan to incorporate the histories of disabled people as an integral part of people's histories as a whole, and the clear commitment to make the building and displays as accessible as possible to disabled people. Colchester Museums recognises that by focusing on the barriers experienced by disabled people, the museum service will improve the quality of access for everyone.

In 1999, Colchester Museums formed an access advisory group, now known as Portal, whose members have been drawn from the local disabled community. The group works with the museum service to assess the displays and facilities to improve physical and intellectual access. The Hollytrees redevelopment project was one of the first projects with Portal's involvement. Their contributions included

The blocked arcade, March 1999, proposed for the new museum entrance

assessing the lift in terms of its use, advising on the surface finish for the access ramp and devising a tassel as a simple and elegant solution for opening doors for those with limited reach.

The redevelopment proposals were discussed with the Heritage Lottery Fund (HLF) at an early stage to ensure that they were suitable for funding. The bid was successful and an award of £369,000 was made in December 1999. In the end, the total project cost amounted to £660,000, owing to increases in the building works, the shortfall being met by an increased contribution from Colchester Borough Council funds. The redevelopment took 15 months, from May 2000 to July 2001. Purcell Miller Tritton and Brennan and Whalley were retained, both playing crucial creative and supervisory roles.

The new displays have as their theme domestic life and childhood in Colchester over the last 300 years. The research into Hollytrees, to make the case for listed building consent, has also been used in the displays to tell the story of the house and those who lived and worked there. The interpretive treatment has sought to maintain the integrity and dignity of the

interiors of the house by acknowledging the architectural features in each room and the historic purposes of the various spaces. The only room in which the original architectural features have not been highlighted is in the Childhood Gallery where the interpretation focuses on the museum displays. The floor of this room also hides a massive steel beam, discovered during the opening-up work. It was left in place and an up-and-over ramp was incorporated into the design of the Childhood Gallery. This approach has been effective as the rising and falling floor level fits well with the magical feel of the displays in this room.

A variety of display methods were used in order to allow as wide an audience as possible intellectual access to the collections. There is use of sound, smell, interactive exhibits and objects to handle on open display, as well as glass-case displays. Where sound stores are used, typed transcripts are provided and audiovisuals are subtitled. The displays themselves are rich in objects, and extensive use of photographs and of personal testimony from the archive of Colchester Recalled, the local oral-history society, has been made to ensure that the displays are rooted in the town.

Accessible information is also provided away from the displays. Thorough information on how to reach Hollytrees Museum and a description of facilities has been produced in large print, Braille and on audiotape. This allows disabled people to make a judgment on whether a visit will be suitable for them. Royal National Institute of the Blind (RNIB) maps for all have been placed in the entrance and on the first floor landing to help orientate visitors around the museum. The colour contrast, plan in relief and use of Braille on these maps does make them easy to use for all visitors and again fulfils the spirit of the inclusive approach enshrined in the DDA.

Attention has been given to representation of disabled people in the museum displays. The approach has been to integrate their life stories throughout the themes of domestic life and childhood, as is the case in reality. Examples include the audio point in the *Running the Home* room where Mrs Hilliard, who went blind in her late teens, discusses her domestic arrangements, and the text panel describing the life of John Vine, a successful 19th century local artist born with virtually no arms, that accompanies his portrait of the Phillips family children in the Childhood Gallery.

The video of the British Sign Language version of the poem, *Twinkle, Twinkle, Little Star*, that runs in the Childhood Gallery is the result of a project funded by the Millennium Festival that saw the museum service working in partnership with other organisations and the local deaf community. The project has been an excellent vehicle for the museum to initiate a relationship with the deaf community who had previously felt that Colchester Museums had nothing of interest for them. The relationship has been sustained with further events and the presence of the Twinkle video has encouraged repeat visits to Hollytrees.

The aim of the redevelopment was to increase the annual visitor figures to 30,000 during the first four years, and then to sustain it at that level. The target audiences for Hollytrees were family groups with pre-school and primary school-age children, older residents and disabled people.

The redevelopment has succeeded on all these fronts. Visitor numbers topped 39,000 for 2003/04 including 3,500 schoolchildren. Within the overall figure are a substantial number of repeat visits by local residents, including, unexpectedly, many teenagers. The lift has been of wide benefit not only to those with

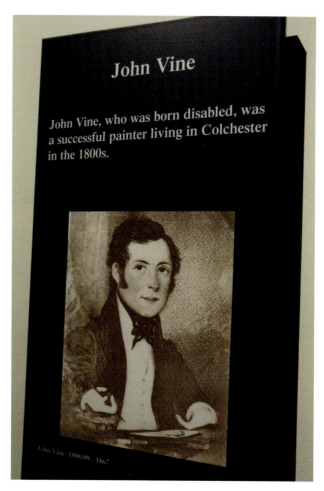

Display panel for John Vine

restricted mobility, but to other people as well, such as those with pushchairs. A survey carried out in the month after the museum opened revealed a satisfaction rating of 99 per cent. The redevelopment has received awards from Colchester Civic Society, the East of England Tourist Board and the Association for Heritage Interpretation. At the heart of the success of Hollytrees Museum is an ongoing process of evaluation focusing on access for all.

English Heritage's account

by Andrew Derrick, English Heritage (now with The Architectural History Practice Ltd)

Hollytrees Museum is housed in a fine, early 18th century former town house in the centre of Colchester. It lies close to Colchester Castle, which is built over the site of the Roman Temple of Claudius, and which is now the centrepiece of a public park, Castle Park. It is

Vine's painting of The Phillips Children

an area of rich archaeological, architectural and townscape significance. Hollytrees Museum is a Grade I listed building, the area around it (and beneath it) is scheduled as an Ancient Monument, and Castle Park is on the English Heritage Register of Parks and Gardens of special historic interest in England. The site lies within the town centre conservation area.

Hollytrees was built in 1719 by Thomas Blagden, a London builder, for Elizabeth Cornelison of Camberwell. It is a handsome, brick town house with a frontage of five bays. There is a central doorway approached by a flight of steps. In 1748, a west extension was built by the local architect James Deane for Charles Gray, who as well as being MP and a JP, was a prominent antiquary. His mother-in-law had kindly bought him Colchester Castle as a wedding present, the Castle thereby becoming part of the garden setting of Hollytrees. This must be regarded as the ultimate Georgian garden building or folly.

Prior to the recent alterations, the main entrance to Hollytrees was at the stone flight of steps at the front of the building (see photo on p 55). There was a panelled entrance hall, in which were located the reception desk and a small shop. From the hall, a fine original staircase runs to the full height of the building, the landings giving onto the display rooms, many of which retain original panelling, fireplaces and other notable historic features. The half landings connect to the rooms in Deane's extension.

The architectural qualities of the building were beyond question; equally apparent were the drawbacks of the building in terms of its current use, and in particular in terms of its accessibility. The main entrance was from the flight of steps at the front, with a wheelchair access at the side giving very limited access to the interior. There was no lift, and there was the challenge of the different floor levels in the extension relative to the main accommodation.

Improving accessibility as far as could reasonably be achieved was not only a legal requirement, but was also, of course, desirable in principle. There was also a desire to consider afresh the presentation and display of the museum. However, it was clear that given the

Original entrance to Hollytrees on the south side

constraints, any works of alteration would need to be handled with the utmost care and sensitivity.

Local authorities are required to notify English Heritage of all applications involving alterations to Grade I and Grade II* listed buildings. These are buildings of particular architectural and historic importance, and together represent about seven per cent of the national stock of listed buildings. Sadly, we are often only consulted when plans are in an advanced stage of development, at which time negotiation of major amendments is often difficult. To its credit, Colchester Borough Council and Purcell Miller Tritton, their appointed architects, approached English Heritage at an early stage, and the project was developed in a spirit of positive cooperation and partnership. English Heritage support was necessary not only to secure the necessary statutory consents, but also on account of our role as advisers to the HLF, from whom the Borough were seeking substantial grant aid.

From the start, the quality and importance of the building and its setting were recognised by all parties. So too was the clear need to adapt the building to make it more accessible and attractive to a whole range of visitors. There was a desire to relocate the main entrance to the museum away from the front door to the rear of the building, which gave onto Castle Park. Apart from the obvious advantages of this in terms of access (level access could be provided at the rear), it was anticipated (correctly as it turns out) that an entrance from a popular and well-used park would encourage more people into the building.

English Heritage often takes a dim view about shifting the entrance to a historic building away from the traditional point of entry, especially in a museum or country house context, since this can alter the sense of the building's layout, and a clear understanding of the function and hierarchy of different rooms and spaces. However, there are sometimes practical advantages in doing so, and sometimes there are also advantages for the historic building and its presentation. In this case, the decision to relocate the entrance to the rear allowed for the re-opening of an original brick loggia/arcade on the garden elevation by the removal of some unsympathetic infilling dating from the 19th century and later. This was replaced with a glass screen set behind the arches, a simple and unapologetically modern solution which allowed some sense of the openness of the loggia to be reinstated in the view from the park. The York stone floor in the new entrance lobby matches that outside the building, and increases the sense of reversion to a semi-outdoor area. A further advantage of relocating the entrance was that it allowed the reception area and shop to be relocated away from the original entrance hall, thus effecting a welcome improvement in the presentation of that important space (see photo of front hall below).

Provision of a lift was more difficult. An original suggestion was that a new external lift structure might be bolted onto the side – the east elevation. This elevation was not of particular architectural distinction (another building, demolished in the 1930s had abutted it, and its most distinguishing feature was the Virginia creeper that covered it). However, this location was inconveniently distanced from the proposed new entrance on the west side of the building, and on account of the differing floor levels in the 1719 house and the 1748 extension, would still have left major circulation and access difficulties. Furthermore, English Heritage considered that an external lift shaft would have an undesirable visual impact externally. While it was therefore clear to all parties that an internal solution was desirable, it was not at all clear that the constraints of the fabric would allow for this.

However, following further documentary research and analysis of the building fabric, a satisfactory solution did present itself. There

was an area between the original house and the 1748 west wing, which had been much altered in the 1920s, following acquisition of the building by Colchester Corporation and its conversion to a museum. It was clear that this area had lost any historic features of any significance and although a tight fit, it proved possible to insert a lift shaft here. This would be accessible from the new lobby area and would give access both to the ground and first floors of the 1719 house, and to the first and second floors of the 1748 extension. A certain amount of shaving back and reconstruction of masonry was needed in this area, but generally this was an area already disturbed in the 1920s.

There was, however, a difficulty. On the first floor of the 1719 house, the formation of a door from the lift to the room housing the childhood display meant breaking through the panelling that lined the walls of this room. Normally this would be regarded as problematic, given the Grade I listing, but careful analysis of the fabric demonstrated that the panelling had in fact been already altered at the time of the 1920s adaptations. Given the clear advantages of locating the lift here, and the fact that this could after all be achieved with little or no loss of significant historic fabric, English Heritage was happy to agree to this change. However, we suggested that the panelling should be adapted to form a flush or 'gib' door, so that when the door was closed the appearance of continuous panelling was essentially preserved. Such doors are commonly found in Georgian houses where there is a wish to underplay an opening. It might be thought there was a conflict at Hollytrees between the conservation demand to make this adaptation as inconspicuous as possible, and the practical need to ensure that

Hollytrees Museum includes many old domestic articles which can be handled by children

Interesting hands-on display of domestic objects at Hollytrees

Lift door closed

the door was visible to those who were likely to need it. However, this has been resolved by discreet signing and appropriate management.

The upgrading and adaptation of Hollytrees involved much more than responding to the requirements of the DDA. A fundamental rethink of the presentation of the display has taken place, and the opportunity taken to remove a number of unsympathetic (but reversible) displays and partitions. The fact that redecoration and upgrading needed to take account of fire regulations is another story in itself. However, with careful thought and wide consultation, it has proved possible to transform Hollytrees, while preserving the special interest of the listed building and enhancing its presentation. The success of the scheme demonstrates the value of early consultation with advisory bodies such as English Heritage, and of ensuring that the priorities of all parties are identified and wherever possible reconciled at an early stage. It also demonstrates the value of what we call 'informed conservation', whereby building

Lift door in use

analysis and recording precedes and informs the development of proposals. The result is a better understood, better looking and more accessible museum for Colchester.

Architect's account

by Simon Marks, Project Manager, Purcell Miller Tritton

Introduction

Hollytrees was constructed in 1718 and is fairly typical of an early Georgian House with red brick façades trimmed with gauged rubbed brickwork to the windows and corner pilasters. In 1748, the house was extended on the west elevation with a two-storey west wing. Due to the floors of the new wing gaining access from the half landings of the principal staircase, the floor levels in the wing and the original building do not coincide. This feature was to become significant in the building's later use.

Prior to 1926, the house had always been used as a private residence and had been adapted by successive owners in often subtle ways, very few of which were formally recorded, and because of the considerable social changes in the 200 years following construction, it is difficult to say that the use of the rooms in 1926 necessarily reflected their original use. When the house was converted to a museum in 1926, its top floor became a flat for the curator, the floors below being display areas. In the 1960s, the flat was removed, the upper part of the building was used as storage and archive areas, and many of the display spaces were remodelled.

In 1995, the Borough Council commissioned an access audit of the museum and its immediate surroundings. Access was severely restricted due to the layout of the existing building. The principal entrance door on the street elevation was 750mm above the general paving level. Only three rooms on the original ground floor were accessible from the level of the principal entrance and access to all other rooms was subject to negotiation of further flights of stairs. The west wing contained an alternative access point on the north elevation, approximately 150mm above the garden ground levels, but this entrance only gave access to two rooms in the ground floor level of the west wing.

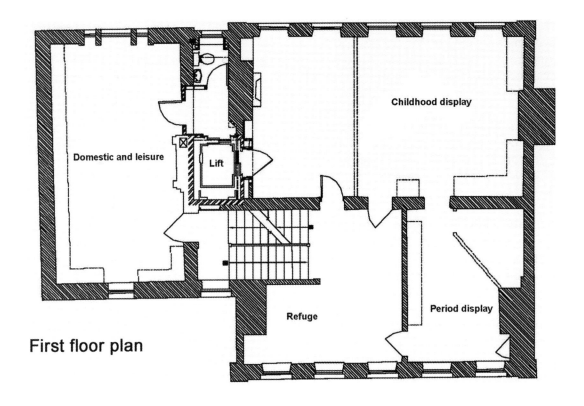

First floor plan

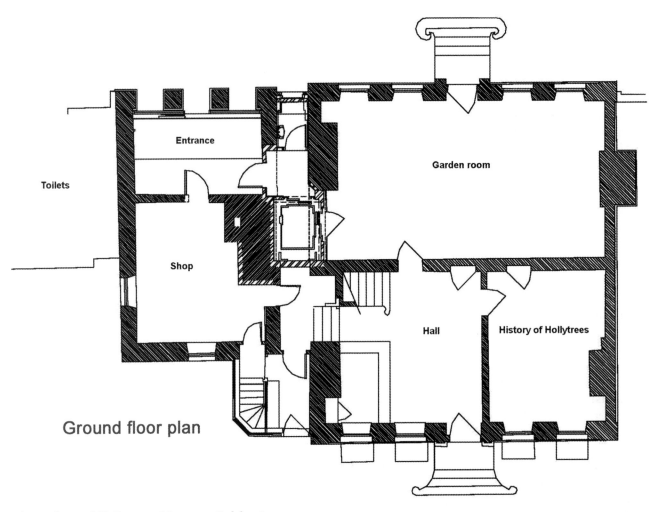

Ground floor plan

Floor plans of Hollytrees Museum, Colchester

It was apparent that in order to apply the recommendations of the access audit, significant alterations to the building would be required. Hollytrees Museum is Grade I listed and alteration would require listed building consent. In 1997, Purcell Miller Tritton were commissioned by the Borough Council to advise on methods of achieving the aspirations of the access audit in an architecturally sensitive manner with minimum intervention in the historic fabric.

An initial assessment of the building suggested that providing access for disabled people to all of the existing accommodation would severely compromise the historic fabric, and that therefore efforts should be concentrated on providing access to the principal display areas of the museum, namely the ground and first floors of the house and west wing.

Initial design studies

Prior to assessing potential positions for access improvements, a general assessment was made of the structure to consider its general condition and the extent to which the individual areas had been altered in the 20th century works to convert the house to a museum.

The study showed that rooms on the ground floor and the second floor of the main block, and on the first floor of the west wing, had had the least alterations. The first floor of the main block had had a considerable number of alterations and the 18th century plan was indistinct. The majority of the interventions had taken place in the 19th century, and those from the 20th century were easily recognisable and could be reversed comparatively easily.

The greatest interventions had been in the ground floor of the west wing and the narrow service section between the west wing and the main house. This wing had originally contained the closets for the house, and after addition of the west wing it had contained service rooms and a very narrow servants' stair. In 1926, the servants' stair had been removed and each level used as toilet accommodation. On a number of floors, the existing floors had been replaced with reinforced concrete.

In the ground floor of the west wing, the surviving design drawings for the building indicated the presence of an open loggia with service facilities to the north. By the late 20th century this loggia had been filled in and the space used as service accommodation for the museum, with numerous modern additions. However, there were indications on the surface that this area contained the remains of earlier links between the main building and the west wing.

Means of escape

The house is of a relatively modest size and it had not been thought necessary on conversion to introduce a fire escape into the building. Consequently all vertical circulation above ground floor level was dependent on the single original staircase which opened directly onto the entrance hall (one of the best preserved parts of the original building), and there was no possibility of isolating the staircase from other rooms.

In introducing the means for disabled people to gain access to the upper floors, it would also be necessary to provide a means of evacuating them in the event of an emergency. It was apparent from very early on that fire escape improvements would have to form part of the accessibility improvements. The layout of the building made it impractical for a new staircase to be accommodated internally. Consultations took place with the fire brigade and English Heritage to consider the possibility in principle of introducing an additional staircase and possibly a lift.

The most likely position for a new vertical circulation structure was the west gable. This part of the building had not received much attention in the original design owing to its abutment with an adjoining property which was removed after the First World War. The provision of a new vertical circulation tower would be practical as it would be visible from the street and garden frontage; however, due to the half levels, it would not provide wheelchair access to the first floor of the west wing – possibly the most architecturally rewarding space in the building. The consultations with English Heritage and the fire brigade suggested that the provision of an additional structure would present particular conservation concerns and should be regarded as a last resort. The fire brigade felt that with fire separation of the individual rooms, and the addition of a more sophisticated sensor and alarm system, it would be possible to provide a viable means of escape via the existing staircase.

With an apparent resolution of escape concerns, the principal problem remained that a location would have to be found within the building for a lift. The positioning required two criteria to be considered:

■ a position which provided access to the maximum number of rooms

■ a position avoiding disturbance to the principal historic and architectural features

Ancillary access problems

The report by Earnscliffe Davies had identified 26 issues that needed attention to improve access for disabled people. The principal items raising architectural issues were:

■ the provision of safety barriers around the light-wells to the front of the house

■ the provision of safety railings around the rear light-well

■ a ramped entrance

■ an entrance hall counter and reception suitable for disabled people

■ an improved fire exit and a refuge area on each floor for wheelchair users

■ a lift to the first floor

Solutions to some of these problems were relatively straightforward and identified early in the design process: for example, the front light-wells provided with gratings that continued to allow light and air in, but provided a safe surface for visitors to walk on.

The rear light-well was protected with a balustrade, the design of which was based on the existing handrails to the garden entrance of the house. Safe refuges could be provided on each floor level of the staircase by modest rearrangements of the displays.

The existing entrance counter had been installed in the 1960s and was of no historic value. Modification would be relatively easy. However, the design team felt that its position in the main entrance hall and proximity to the main staircase was architecturally unsatisfactory and it would be preferable if the entrance counter could be located in an alternative position, leaving the entrance hall in its intended architectural form.

The remaining two problems were the major issues: the provision of a ramp to the entrance and the provision of a lift. Providing an entrance ramp to the front entrance was considered to be architecturally unsatisfactory by the design team, and English Heritage had indicated that they would not approve such a proposal. The existing entrance had a fine staircase to an ornate door, and the provision of a ramp would lead to the loss of the staircase and would architecturally dominate the frontage of the house.

Locating the lift

The survey of the house had indicated that the most disturbed section of the building was the narrow link between the west wing and the main block. However, the positioning of a lift in this space did not overcome the fact that the ground floor entrance was some 1200mm above the general garden level and a further means of access would be required to the base of the lift. The initial thought was to provide a lift stop at the ground floor of the west wing, but because of the half level involved, the lift would require entrance doors on alternate sides, which takes up slightly more space than a single-sided entrance lift. This was to provide further technical problems as the shaft available for the lift was only 1500mm wide.

In the feasibility study commissioned by the Borough Council, the design team became more and more convinced that the solution lay in relocating the principal entrance to the building. Although the west wing entrance option involved considerable alteration to the use of the building, it offered a solution that was less architecturally intrusive.

The existing approach to the south side of the building was via a relatively sharp slope climbing out of a natural dip in the grounds of the park. Checking of the levels indicated that with a modest re-alignment of one path within Castle Park, an approach could be provided conforming to ramp standards for wheelchair access. This approach offered an additional advantage in that adjacent to the west wing of the house were the park toilets, including an existing wheelchair accessible toilet.

Although the principle of an entrance on the garden side of the building was relatively straightforward, the exact form of the entrance was more of a problem. The existing garden entrance to the main house was unsuitable, and the servants' entrance door on the garden elevation still involved a change of level. Also, the door case was unsuitable for conversion. The arched openings of the loggia still existed; however, they had been glazed with full-height sash windows. Analysis of these windows showed that the historic fabric was a 1960s intervention and could be removed without significant loss. More of a problem was the overall height of the openings, which were less than two metres above the existing, internal floor levels. It would be necessary to lower the floor level within the building in order to provide adequate headroom. The additional room needed was modest, about 150mm; however, this would involve an internal ramp in the building to get back to the existing floor levels within the ground floor of the west wing.

An architectural solution was found involving frameless glass infill panels to the rear of the deep reveals of the loggia, with an automatic door in the central opening giving access to a lobby with a ramped floor. The new entrance would be located within the room to the south of the lobby conveniently positioned to the proposed lift location.

Sizing the lift

The internal lift option involved four stops which would provide access to the ground and first floor in the west wing and ground and first floor in the main block. Due to the half levels in the house, some of the lift car stops were less than a metre apart which required the use of a lift with doors on alternate sides. Initially, the idea was to place the car doors opposite each other to avoid the need to manoeuvre a wheelchair within the lift. However, this would severely restrict the location of the openings for lift access in the first floor room in the west wing. It was eventually resolved that the entrances to the lift car should be on adjoining sides so that the existing service rooms became lobbies, allowing a more sensitive location of the entrance doors in the first floor of the west wing. Unfortunately, the use of adjoining side entrance doors increased the size of the lift car on both axes.

At the time of the scheme, the minimum recommended size for a lift for a wheelchair user, with an adjoining entrance lobby to the lift, was possible within the space available. However, during detailed design it became apparent that this would not be entirely

satisfactory as wheelchair users with helpers would find it difficult to negotiate the 90° change of direction within the lift car. Unfortunately, the desirable size for the lift car could not be accommodated without affecting the wall surfaces in either the first floor of the west wing room or the room on the first floor of the main block. Further discussion with English Heritage indicated that a lift penetrating into either of the rooms would not be acceptable because of the extent of the disturbance of the architectural features such as cornices and panelling. After very careful surveying of the building, including opening up of the structure to check the method of construction, a compromise size was agreed which provided the maximum available space within the car, while removing the minimum amount of brickwork within the shaft and avoiding disturbance of the panelled finishes within the rooms.

Due to the dimensional sensitivity of the overrun, it had been established early on that the lift would need to be hydraulically operated, with the motor room located in the existing basement of the main block. A lift manufacturer was brought in to assist the detailed design at an early stage, and to some extent the design of the lift car could be adjusted to maximise the amount of space available within the car. The space available was so restricted that the historic settlement of the building was an issue. If the walls to the west or east of the shaft had been significantly

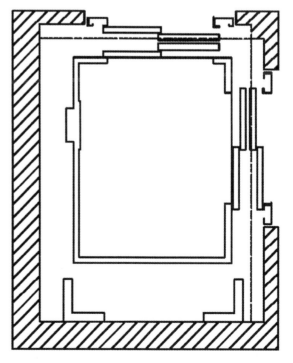

Plan of lift showing doors on adjacent sides

out of plumb, this would have reduced the effective width of the shaft, possibly at a critical position. To determine this, the concrete floors of the existing toilets were core-drilled to provide a position to lower a plumb line through the full height of the building and to check the offsets of the walls.

It was decided to create gib doors exploiting the Georgian design vocabulary for creating unobtrusive doors in panelled rooms. Positioning the door controls was more difficult. The matter was resolved by partially recessing the controls behind a hinged flap of moulding, allowing the panelling to be restored to its correct appearance if the lift is not in use.

Other works

The initial feasibility study had indicated that the ground floor of the west wing could have a more ancient level of finishes concealed behind the 20th century plaster. An archaeological investigation was carried out

and the remains of an external door opening of the 1719 house was discovered in the wall between the main block and the ground floor level in the west wing. It proved possible to open up this doorway to provide a link through from the new entrance area to the base of the main staircase.

As part of the access improvements, the museum collection was re-displayed, the design of the new display being carried out by Brennan and Whalley. This allowed signage to be improved and more space to be provided around exhibits for wheelchair users.

The removal of old glass cabinets allowed the full architectural splendour of the principal rooms to be revealed, and offered the possibility of restoring an authentic colour scheme to the walls and ceilings. In selected rooms, notably the ground floor hall and the first floor southeast room, the architectural detail of the rooms became part of the display, with themed displays of artefacts relevant to the date of the room. The existing paint finishes on the wall were investigated in the

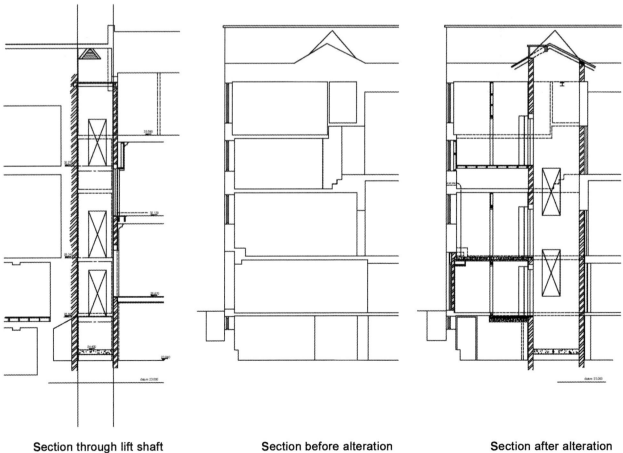

Section through lift shaft   Section before alteration   Section after alteration

Sections through Hollytree Museum

hope that an original colour scheme could be identified and copied. However, the results were inconclusive, and colour schemes typical of the period illustrated in each room were chosen.

Conclusion

The project was particularly satisfying to work on, as it ultimately proved possible to fully meet the client's requirement for improvements to the building and the museum and in a way that enhanced the existing architecture of the historic fabric. To achieve such a result needed a client body committed to fully understanding the building and carrying out adequate research to progress a solution that, in the early stages, appeared controversial. This illustrates that a comprehensive and scholarly knowledge of a building can lead a design team to access solutions that enhance the original architecture rather than disguise it.

© Jonathan Goldberg

Old front hall, now uncluttered with ancillary services

Towneley Hall aerial view

Towneley Hall Museum, Burnley

Client:	Towneley Hall Museum
Architect:	Burnley Borough Council
Access Consultant:	Brian Towers RIBA NRAC Consultant

Overview

by Adrian Cave

This large Grade I listed country house, which dates partly from the 15th century, is surrounded by a large, wooded park and has long been appreciated by local residents. Although access was restricted by steps and stairs and by the lack of a lift, some local people were strongly opposed to any changes to the building before the project for improved access and facilities was carried out.

The new extension provides step-free access via a new entrance to the new reception area and a shop, freeing the historic building from these activities. Ingenious changes to a corridor, which formerly had three steps and is now a long, sloping corridor, provide improved access to several rooms and easier access and circulation routes for everyone. It may be noted that, although this ramp has a gradient of 1:18 and no handrails, this appears to have caused few problems. A new lift provides access to the rooms and displays at the first and second floor levels, in the existing Hall.

Analysis of the history of a building is essential before any alterations are made to improve accessibility, and a thorough investigation was carried out at Towneley Hall. This helped to identify a much-altered tower as being an admirable location for the new lift. It was,

therefore, sheer bad luck that the trial holes failed to reveal that the foundations of the tower were not just under the walls, as would normally be expected, but also under the middle of the tower, and that the construction of the lift pit would undermine these foundations and result in unforeseen additional costs.

Some rooms, such as the Priest's Hiding Hole, are not accessible to those who cannot use stairs. However, there is an interactive computer display which is operated by selecting a number on a marked plan and obtaining a selection of pictures and information on the screen. This is an effective demonstration of how to provide information in ways which help to make the exhibits and services of the Museum more accessible.

There is an interesting example of the difficulties in reconciling the requirements of conservation with those of display. In a display of church vestments, which for conservation reasons are exhibited with very low levels of illumination, the route towards the Chapel leads directly towards a window. This causes considerable problems of glare, even for people without impaired vision. The situation could be improved if a screen were to be provided between the exhibits and the Chapel in order to reduce the problems of glare in the dimly lit exhibition space and to allow time for the eye to adjust to the different levels of illumination.

© Kit Smith

The previous front entrance façade

The popularity of the Museum for school groups appears to have exceeded expectations, and as a result the WC provision tends to be very busy at peak times. At the time of the author's visit, the mirror in the only accessible WC was from a height of about 1100–1500mm above floor level, which is too high for wheelchair users. This is a variation on a common problem in accessible WCs where the mirror, designed specifically for wheelchair users, is often no higher than about 1000mm and is too low for many other people who make use of accessible WCs. These include many visually impaired people who find that standard accessible WCs are useful because the layout is more predictable than in other WCs.

Externally, the house has extensive grounds, with natural ground slopes which sometimes exceed 1:20. The main car park has about eight designated spaces for disabled people, although the markings on the tarmac were largely obscured at the time of the visit. The car park is more than 400m from the house, but because the distances and gradients could cause problems, disabled people are permitted to park close to the entrance, where there is step-free access into the building.

The signage to and within the grounds is inconsistent and often unclear, but there are many seats along the paths throughout the site. Improved signage, including maps, would assist visitors to find and enjoy the many attractive features at the site, including the Natural History Centre and Bowling Green, as well as the extensive gardens and woodland.

Client's account

by Susan Bourne, Curator

The history of the museum

Towneley Hall was the home of the Catholic Towneley family for over 500 years. The building stands in a park on the outskirts of the industrial town of Burnley and is bordered on three sides by the hills of northeast Lancashire.

Extensive seating in the Hall grounds

The first building on the site dates from the early 15th century and is now embedded in a variety of later alterations. At one time, the house formed a quadrangle with a gatehouse and must have appeared like an Oxford college. Today, there are three wings entered by an impressive, early 18th century baroque entrance hall with giant pilasters, leading to a Regency drawing room and dining room and an Elizabethan Long Gallery in one wing, and three floors containing servants' quarters, bedrooms, a chapel, a small dining room and two large 20th century art galleries.

One hundred years ago, the last resident, Lady O'Hagan (née Towneley), sold the house, with no contents, to the County Borough of Burnley to become the town's art gallery and museum. The building has always been an important part of the experience for visitors, and in the early 20th century it was filled with loan exhibitions while a permanent collection was built up. It now contains everything you would expect in a medium-sized local museum, from Egyptian mummies to Victorian paintings of ancient Egypt. Gradually, more of the house has been opened to the public, and today,

visitors can see almost all the building either by self-guided visits using a printed guide, or a sound guide, or through a guided tour.

Various architects and builders have worked at Towneley extending and demolishing sections of the building, including John Carr of York in the 1770s and Sir Jeffry Wyatville in the early 19th century. In the 20th century, adaptations to an art gallery and museum were undertaken by the architects' section of Burnley Borough Council.

During Lady O'Hagan's time, the building had become dilapidated in parts, but in the 20th century the local authority spent considerable sums each year adapting and maintaining the building, so that by the 1990s it was in good overall condition. The family bedrooms were replaced with two top-lit art galleries in 1901 and 1924, and these were refurbished twice. Circulation was improved by creating new doorways, but there were no other major internal structural alterations. A rather ramshackle wing containing a dairy and gardener's quarters probably dating from the 18th and 19th centuries was demolished in

The Great Hall

1928. In the 1960s, a flat-roofed lavatory block was built on the site.

It was the poor state of this block that provided the original impetus to improve the facilities in the 1990s. Visitors to the country house and art gallery and museum were justifiably complaining about the dank state of the lavatories. A new pitched-roof toilet extension was costed at £45,000 – a considerable sum for the authority to find in pre-Lottery days.

The project context

In 1996, the Museum was left a bequest of £120,000 by a Burnley man, William Furclough, who had emigrated to Canada. This allowed a more detailed analysis of the needs of the museum service, and soon after, the advent of the National Lottery Fund allowed a really radical Towneley Hall Development Plan.

Consultation with stakeholders confirmed that although the building and its services were much loved, facilities were tired and access was poor. Displays were in need of renewal, and the increasing use of computers meant that staff offices could no longer be tucked into old bedrooms and butler's pantries, where the wiring was inadequate. The Curator also anticipated that local government funding in the future would be under pressure and that income-generating activities such as conferences, weddings and a good shop would be needed.

The brief was to secure the long-term future of Towneley Hall by improving facilities and access. The process of drawing up the plan and obtaining the funding took from 1995 to 2001, and the implementation period from November 2001 to August 2002.

A team was led by the Curator and included Burnley Borough Council staff and consultants and advisors from the North West

Museum Service. Burnley Borough Council's in-house architects' section was used for design and management of the building process. On the advice of the HLF monitor, an outside consultant acted as project manager and an outside design manager was appointed to work with the curatorial team on displays.

Although Towneley Hall had been changed by almost every generation of the Towneley family, it had remained almost unaltered in the 20th century, so any building work would be controversial. Wide consultation early in the process was to be the key to an acceptable and successful scheme. English Heritage, The Civic Trust, The Georgian Group, staff, elected members, visitors, family members, architectural historians, local societies and focus groups were among those involved.

The Curator worked with Terry Preston of the Architects' section of Burnley Council on the initial brief and outline design.

The client brief

The client brief for the new wing was to replace the existing lavatory block to the west of Towneley Hall with a wing based on the former servants' wing demolished in 1928. This should reflect local vernacular styles and materials, as evidenced in surviving outbuildings at Gawthorpe Hall, Padiham; Pendle Heritage Centre, Barrowford; and Towneley Hall. It needed to provide a ground floor link to Towneley Hall in addition to providing a number of visitor facilities, including lavatories, a shop, a library, offices, storage facilities and a lecture room. It was also necessary to minimise the impact of the new wing on the original historic structure.

New displays were required to be provided in Towneley Hall which would interpret the history of the Towneley family and servants, the architecture of Towneley Hall, and the life of a country house using figures from Towneley history and based on recent research by David Eastwood and Susan Bourne. Additional displays should interpret the permanent fine and decorative arts collections and new acquisitions.

Interpretation should be accessible to both adults and children, and should meet the needs of everyone, including disabled people. Environmental, lighting and security conditions should be appropriate for each type of object, which may range from documents and paintings to ceramics and glass.

The curator and architect visited nearby halls and country houses that had retained their servants' quarters for inspiration, and used a pen and ink drawing of the demolished wing as a starting point for a new extension. Later in the project, a photograph was found which showed that this wing had not been the neat building in the drawing, but in fact had been a haphazard collection of buildings.

At this point, access was considered in its widest form. The old building was full of steps and staircases, so physical access was a priority. A lift would be needed, but intellectual access to the displays, and consideration for visually impaired people were also important. Colour schemes, interpretation and content of the displays were checked for accessibility and compliance with current recommendations and good practice.

Towneley is a Grade I listed building, so there were considerable constraints on changes to the building and the curator was keen that physical changes to the building were kept to a minimum. Inserting lifts into the building was a problem and the fresh pair of eyes of the outside design consultant, Alan Robinson, formerly of the North West Museum Service, found an unobtrusive and practical location for the main lift by removing the water closets from a tower built in the 1850s.

The cost of the scheme was now approaching the £1.2 million mark, and the HLF was to be the main funder, with contributions from Lancashire's Single Regeneration Budget for Tourism, The Towneley Hall Society, The North West Museums Service, bequest funds and donations.

However, the scheme ran into considerable opposition from English Heritage, the local Civic Trust, the Georgian Group and the local planners. Where concerns were expressed, they were considered and answered. For example, English Heritage wanted to know why the footprint of the old wing had been chosen for the site of the new extension. The answer was that all other façades would have been damaged by an extension, whereas the traces of the earlier extension remained on the rather muddled north façade, and the new building would sit politely behind the 1850s tower and an ancient tree. The planners felt the new extension should express what it contained. It was pointed out that this was a shop, public lavatories, lecture theatre and offices, which explained the blank walls.

The scheme was submitted to the HLF with only one lift included in the new wing. They required further access improvements. Help was sought from access consultant, Brian Towers, who examined the old building with the curator and architects, and looked at the plans for the new extension.

The new extension allowed a level entry to the new facilities and through to the old building. However, once in the old building, the visitor was met with a variety of different floor levels and steps. The Georgian Group had already suggested raising the floor level of one early 18th century room that was reached by steps down from the doorways.

Brian Towers pointed out that the new extension included a set of steps over the ground floor archway, which could be designed out by raising the roof level of the whole building. For the curator, this also produced a roof space which could be provided with a floor and used as a store. In the main building he designed a route through the servants' area around the kitchen, which was to be opened up to the public. By lifting the existing stone flags and re-laying them on a gentle slope, the need for ramps was eliminated. In fact, there are no ramps in the building and the only area not accessible by wheelchair is the Long Gallery. Most of the alterations are remarkably unobtrusive and many visitors do not realise they have been made.

Another problem was solved by inserting a small wheelchair platform lift in an area of the kitchen. This is the most obtrusive change and the curator accepted it with reluctance as the only solution. The area of the kitchen has been reduced, but existing panelling and up-boards have been reincorporated in the design. It is certainly well used by many appreciative visitors.

The main lift blends in well with the existing building. It is in the servants' area, and the 19th century colour scheme has been extended to the lift casing so that it looks as if it has been there for a long time (if one ignores the brushed steel doors).

The one area it was not possible to provide a lift for was the Long Gallery. It was decided that present budgets would not allow the inclusion of a walk-through platform lift that could be used for emergency evacuation, but that a solution might be available in the

Existing stone flags to the corridor re-laid to a shallow gradient and providing level access to a series of display rooms

future. The stone, cantilever staircase up to the Long Gallery which dates from the 1720s and has a fine wrought-iron balustrade, was not felt to be suitable for a wheelchair platform stairlift. This remains the problem that we have not fully solved.

The bid, including improved access in the main hall, was re-submitted to the HLF and this time was successful.

The outcome and feedback

The brief was met, and we now attract more visitors of all types (up from 98,000 to 130,000 per annum). Comments books and user surveys reveal that the overwhelming number of visitors are very satisfied. However, shortly after the opening, there were complaints from a few visitors and in the local press along the lines of 'don't change Towneley, it has never changed before'. These complaints have now almost completely ceased, as people use and enjoy the building. All visitors have benefited from the changes and most members of staff are pleased with them.

The building now provides a grand, accessible venue with good facilities for weddings and events, which now produce income, helping to solve some of the revenue shortfalls experienced by the museum in the past few years.

The access process

One aspect of the project was making the displays accessible. To do this, we incorporated traditional methods picked up from the National Trust and the new British Galleries at the Victoria and Albert Museum, such as books and albums for people to sit down and read, labels on objects in cases, tie-on labels on furniture and objects for handling. We also included new ideas from other museums such as a virtual tour incorporating inaccessible parts of the building, computer programs showing aspects of the collection and building, sound guides for hire, and models of the building.

Finally, some ideas were our own, including fibre-optic torches to examine objects that needed to be looked at in low light levels, such as textiles, books or information in large print housed in perspex boxes on the side of showcases, and Powerpoint displays on the changing architecture of the building using specially commissioned watercolours of each façade of the building.

We have always attempted to cover a wide variety of topics in the exhibition programme, ranging from the BBC Wildlife Photographer of the Year touring exhibition to the Art of Mountain Biking, created in house. In Burnley, social inclusion and community cohesion are current issues, and exhibitions in the future will need to address these areas.

Undoubtedly, the future of the art gallery and the museum lies in providing displays that will appeal to all sections of the community and be accessible to all.

Access consultant's account

by Brian Towers, RIBA, NRAC Consultant

The commission

Towneley Hall is a Grade I listed building that had been open to the public as an art gallery and museum since the early 1900s.

When I was commissioned, Burnley Borough Council was preparing designs for improving the Hall, including a large extension to provide a shop, staff accommodation and a study centre. I was asked to prepare an access report in order to support an application for Lottery funding. My audit was to concentrate on the building elements, existing and proposed, but to exclude the extensive parklands, part of another project, and the museum exhibits themselves.

The access audit and access appraisal

The access audit of the Hall was carried out on 1 October 1997 after I had studied the plans of the proposed extension.

The audit report included all of the usual recommendations, but the access priorities identified during the audit were:

- The public entrance to Towneley Hall was up a flight of steps into the Great Hall, with no possibility of providing an associated ramped or lift alternative.

- There was no wheelchair accessible route from the new extension through the Hall to the Great Hall and other Regency rooms. There was a flight of steps up from the link to the new extension and there were several small level changes between rooms at ground floor level.

- There was no access to the exhibition rooms and art gallery on the upper levels. A possible location for a lift had been identified, but the many changes in level between rooms meant that only very limited access would be available to people unable to climb steps.

- The imposing Long Gallery could not be reached.

- The drawings of the new extension showed a change of level at first floor; this meant that a platform lift had been introduced in order to provide wheelchair access into the library.

Recommendations

In my report I accepted that the main entrance into the Great Hall could not be used by people unable to climb stairs. To quote from the report: 'It should be accepted that wheelchair access to the building is not available at this entrance, on the understanding that an alternative access to the Great Hall will be made as part of the new work. Also, that the entrance provided in the new development will be sufficiently significant to ensure that it is not classed as a secondary route.'

The new entrance was to be created through the new extension and the shop. This meant resolving the problem of level changes within the ground floor of the Hall. The easy bit was ramping a corridor to give access to a number of exhibition rooms (see photo); the main problem was the flight of steps. I suggested modifying an exhibition in the old kitchen by bringing part of the back wall forward and fitting a platform lift behind it. The curator, Susan Bourne, was not amused. However, the proposal was eventually accepted and there is now wheelchair access throughout the ground floor of the Hall and into the Grand Hall and Regency Rooms.

The lift was fitted into a little used space in the tower and, to enable wheelchair users to take advantage of the access to the upper level, the floor of a central room was raised. This eliminated a series of steps and provided wheelchair access to all of the rooms.

The only part of the building still out of reach was the Long Gallery. My proposal for a walk-through platform lift within one of the Regency Rooms was not able to be afforded, and access to the room for those unable to climb stairs is only available on a Virtual Tour.

The change of level at the first floor of the extension was removed by changing the floor level (easy when a building is not yet built).

The architects of Burnley Borough Council responded constructively to my recommendations. The changes I proposed were incorporated into their design and the alterations in the Hall carried out so skilfully that it is difficult to see what has been done. There is still work to do. In my report I had recommended improvements to the entrance into the Grand Hall. These have not been done due to lack of funds.

A new ramp within a deep wall opening provides access to a suite of rooms previously only accessible via steps

Wall panelling brought forward to conceal the platform lift enclosure and to retain the full display area inside the kitchen

The platform lift sits neatly against a backdrop of original building features, including timber wall panelling and a corbelled stone arch

Architect's account

by Andrew Rolfe, Architectural Consultancy Manager, Burnley Borough Council

Towneley Hall extension and alterations

Pevsner describes Towneley Hall as 'the one outstanding monument of Burnley'. This status, together with it being a Grade I listed building, and its position in the surrounding parkland, nestling against the wooded hillside, has been the determining factor in deciding to locate the new extension on the least 'visible' side of the Hall.

This has ensured that the majestic open views of the Hall, from the northeast (front) and southeast (side), are not visually affected by the new extension. From closer up to the Hall, the extension is seen alongside the northwest elevation, so the decision was taken to adopt a more vernacular style, inoffensive to the original Hall, and in the tradition of ancillary buildings around great houses.

The existing Hall has a history of continual, gradual development and remodelling, from its origins in the Middle Ages when it was a courtyard house. In about 1700, the northeast wing was demolished, creating the present 'open-sided courtyard' arrangement. Later, Gibbs re-styled the southwest façade in early Georgian style, and in the Regency period Wyatville re-styled the southeast façade. In Victorian times, the new tower was built on the northwest side, already a tapestry of alterations. The new extension simply continues this tradition, but using the same building materials and style gives continuity to the above changes. This approach enables the new building to sit discreetly alongside the Hall, not compete with it for attention.

Generally, the new building follows the footprint of the old cottages, (previously demolished). In this respect we followed previous generations, who also realised this location was the only place for an extension that would not compromise the appearance of the main buildings.

The design process

The original sketch design was only for the extension (no work was then envisaged in the Hall). This design was never intended to be a reproduction of the previous building, but it included some similar features, such as the barn doors, chamfered mullion windows and slate roof. However, it also included some more 20th century ideas, such as the glass shop window. Remaining servants' wings at nearby Gawthorpe Hall, and the Pendle Heritage Centre, together with their modern solutions to similar problems, were visited.

The extension sitting discreetly alongside the main building

At this point, the design went out for wide consultation and in view of the good support for the scheme; it was then submitted to the HLF in mid-1996.

The HLF undertook a detailed appraisal, including an architectural one, for which they appointed the distinguished architect, John Winter, who said:

'I have to say that I think the designers have done rather well. The proportions of the buildings have considerable charm, the materials are good and the plan sensible' and 'I accept that, if Towneley Hall is to be extended, then this is the place to do it.'

The HLF accordingly gave approval in principle in February 1997. However, the reason for withholding full approval was concern about the museum not having taken the opportunity to improve accessibility in the existing building. I suppose we had, up to then, considered the existing building more or less off limits for any significant alterations.

The HLF advised, but some of their suggestions proved problematic and expensive (for instance, to put a lift in the very narrow and historic tower leading up to the chapel, by fully supporting the exterior face of the walls, and then cutting away the inside thickness of the walls to make enough room for a lift).

Later in 1997, Brian Towers, an architect and access consultant, was appointed to the design team. He worked with us and with the curator, and arrived at the solutions which give access to most parts of the Hall, except the Long Gallery, for which there is now a virtual reality tour.

The revised scheme, including the additional access work in the existing Hall, and also some access and other improvements in the new extension, was re-submitted to the HLF and later, in mid-1999, full funding approval was finally given, so the scheme could then be worked up in more detail, with a detailed planning application.

Details of the design

The new extension, a two-storey, pitched-roof building, linked to the Hall by a single-storey pitched-roof element, both similar in scale to the earlier servants' wing.

The lift and stairs in the new extension are off the foyer that allows a route through the building, from the barn doors on either side. The first floor section provides new exhibition preparation rooms, offices and a kitchen/rest room. This allowed these areas to be removed from the main Hall and the rooms thus vacated were then developed as public rooms,

(Top) 1897 drawing of Towneley to accompany a legal document for the sale of the house to Burnley Corporation, with the servants quarters that were demolished in 1929
(Bottom) Sketch of the new extension – now the logo of the Hall

containing additional displays (see photo). The area over the foyer is a new library/research area, with natural lighting being provided through roof-lights, and it has a gallery level reached via a circular staircase.

The extension as a whole is 'dug into' the adjacent ground levels, to maintain the ground floor at the same level as the adjoining Hall's floor level, and also to lessen the visual impact of the height of new building, which needed extra height to accommodate the lift, even though we used lifts without full motor rooms at the top. This level floor also provides simple entry and access for disabled people to all ground floor areas of the extension (shop, kitchen, toilets, lecture theatre), with the lift to provide wheelchair access to the first floor level. There is an alternative means of escape from the first floor for wheelchair users via a bridge to the adjoining higher ground (behind a retaining wall that makes possible a ground floor level path around the building, for use when the 'barn doors route' is closed).

The abutment of the link to the Hall follows the roof line of the earlier wing, below the Chapel windows, minimising contact with the existing building (as can be seen on the northwest elevation/section on p 76), and this had the effect of limiting the internal height of the shop area, which was recovered by using sloping ceilings supported by traditional timber trusses. The glazed façade of the single-storey link also lightens its external visual impact, when viewed from the side seen by most approaching visitors. The early 20th century doorway and windows to the ground floor of the Hall are enclosed by the link, but retained inside the shop.

Provision of a new lift in part of the Victorian Tower of the existing Hall (that formerly contained dilapidated lavatories) gives wheelchair access up to the Art Gallery at second floor level and the Chapel and display rooms at first floor level (both in the northwest wing). A platform lift in an area of the original kitchen, little seen by the public, provides access for wheelchair users from the lower ground floor level in the northwest wing up to the upper ground level in the main central Hall, and thus on to the Regency Rooms that are at the same level in the southeast wing. Attendant improvements create a wheelchair-friendly route through to

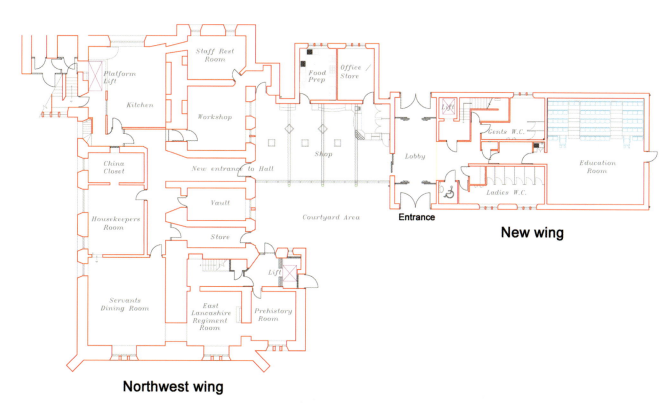

Northwest wing

New wing

Ground floor plan of extension

Elevation, showing abutment of the new wing against the northwest wing

The new entrance to Towneley Hall

both the new lift and to the shop in the new extension, at lower ground floor level in the northwest wing. These include raising the entire floor level in the room then used to exhibit the East Lancashire Regiment material (formerly the Stewards' Room); this in turn involved raising both the fireplace (that had been relocated from Burnley Barracks), and the radiator under the window (which had enough headroom for the new floor level).

The provision of the lift in the Hall involved obscuring (internally) the doorway, with its impressive external 'Gibbs'-style surround, but this door was retained externally and a cupboard formed behind it, so it can be maintained in good order. The windows above this door, including two Georgian windows relocated when the tower was built, were retained externally (but blacked out internally), as part of the new lift shaft. The ground floor Victorian window on the west side of the tower was sympathetically altered to form a new escape door (in place of the Gibbs-style one mentioned above).

This work on site was one of the few areas that caused significant delay and extra cost, as the old foundations of the Victorian tower were found to have been walls stepped down internally, to the point of almost meeting in the middle of the tower (we had only dug a trial pit outside the tower, as it had a solid floor internally). Thus when we formed the lift pit, we were effectively removing the foundations of the Tower, so had then to unexpectedly embark on underpinning, using piled supports.

Alternatives considered

Surprisingly to us, our then conservation architect in the planning department was all in favour of an ultra-modern extension in the early consultations. We thus looked at examples that had been attached to other historic buildings, both 'brutal contrasts' and 'reflective glass' solutions, but failed to find anything that could be fitted comfortably alongside Towneley Hall, let alone anything that did not get an adverse reaction from our client, the Curator, Susan Bourne.

With regard to alternatives for access solutions, we were constrained by the quality of the existing building, and thus the need to minimise any damage to it. Also, by the time that we started looking at improving access in the Hall, the broad level of financial support in the Lottery 'approved in principle' had been determined, so solutions had to be economical. In reality, there were certain 'pinch points' that had to be overcome and there were no practical and affordable alternative solutions to those devised by our helpful access consultant, Brian Towers.

The design team was advised in particular by W John Smith, an architectural historian with specialist knowledge of Towneley Hall. The team included Terry Preston initially, and later Peter Butterfield and John Lyons, from the Architects' section, structural engineer, Paul Sowden and quantity surveyor, Michael Stobbs.

Entrance to Sunderland Museum

 © Jonathan Goldberg

Sunderland Museum and Winter Gardens, Tyne and Wear

Client:	Sunderland Museum and Winter Gardens
Architects:	City of Sunderland
Access Consultant:	Burdus Access Management

Overview

by Adrian Cave

Large 19th century museum buildings are often a formidable challenge when trying to create an atmosphere of welcoming informality. The constraints of classical symmetry may include a flight of imposing entrance steps and a spacious entrance hall, both of impressive but daunting scale. At the Sunderland Museum, a Grade II listed building, these problems have been overcome by construction of a new extension, with an entrance which has become a landmark in the city, and which leads into a bright and informal reception area and shop. From here, a long and gentle internal ramp at about 1:20 leads almost imperceptibly to the main ground floor level, from which a lift provides access to the main upper floors. At the opposite end of the building to the new entrance, the spectacular Winter Gardens provides a climax after the journey through the building.

The Sunderland Museum uses an immense variety of display techniques and is worth a visit merely to study these. They include:

- the sound of a brass band which introduces a display of the life of a former coal-mining community
- a film telling the story of a small boy working in a mine after his father was killed in the same mine
- displays to explain the diseases to which miners were prone
- films and models to illustrate the story of ship-building and other industries which have almost disappeared from the region
- the gigantic prow of a ship which dominates one of the staircases
- at the other end of the scale, small boxes which can be opened to see and touch the contents which include wooden clogs, workmen's tools, fabrics, fossils and dried gourds
- a model of St Peter's Anglo-Saxon Monastery
- display cases of local glass, pottery and prehistoric artefacts
- traditional displays of stuffed birds and animals, but with push buttons to illuminate selected creatures, or to hear recordings of their calls

In a building as large and complicated as the Sunderland Museum, orientation and signage are important if visitors are to be able to find their way around with ease. In this respect there were a number of problems during my visit in January 2004. The list of floor levels and displays outside the lift show the ground floor at the top and the top floor at the bottom, causing unnecessary complications to orientation and wayfinding

The signage systems generally were neither sufficiently clear nor consistent to make it easy for visitors to find their way around. However, visitors are provided with printed floor plans to carry around with them, and the main signboard outside the Museum is clear and informative with a good display of symbols which continues internally to show the principal routes to lifts, WCs, café, and so on. The main ground floor route, Museum 'street', between the entrance at one side and the Winter Gardens on the other provides a recognisable space by which visitors can orientate themselves, and this is enhanced by the height of the hallway through several floor levels, giving views down to the ground floor from various upper levels. The high space and foliage of the Winter Gardens at the east end

are also visible from many levels and are a useful guide, literally, to orientation.

The café is strategically located at ground floor level between the main Galleries and the Winter Gardens, with windows to the latter. With level circulation generally, and adaptable furniture, this provides space for refreshment and relaxation for everyone. Near the main circulation route, a row of seats is much used by older visitors and in a building of this size, seats for people to rest are very desirable. Fortunately, there are three rows of seats in Museum street and seats for visitors in all the galleries.

Since this piece was written, funding has been secured for a range of further improvements, including audio guides and pre-visit guides and a tactile orientation map for the entrance hall.

The Winter Gardens breaks many of the normal rules for accessibility and is all the more interesting for this. A variety of stimulating sensory experiences is provided by the sounds of water, a touch of foliage, warmth of sunlight, smells of flowers and unexpected views. Access into the Winter

© Jonathan Goldberg

Users at an interactive display

Gardens at ground level is via large, automatic, sliding glass doors, then via steps or a ramp with overhanging foliage, to the lower level which is dominated by waterfalls and a pool with colourful fish. To reach this, the visitors pass along a smooth pathway alongside a stream with no tactile warning between path and water. The benefits include the pleasures of being close to the flowing water while the risks of accidents are probably minimal, as the edge of the path is very similar to that of a pavement and, for people with impaired vision, the greatest safeguard is predictability. For those with vision, there are surprises: at intervals, the concrete path shows the paw marks of various creatures which appear to have disappeared into the undergrowth just as the concrete was setting!

A glass lift carries intrepid explorers up to the Gallery at tree-top level. A journey in this fully glazed lift, with only a handrail as visual enclosure, is a stimulating experience for anyone, and the lack of manifestation of the glass seems fully justified. Only those who wish to ride up to the Gallery have any need to do so, and those who choose to do this have an

© Jonathan Goldberg

Walkway across the Winter Gardens

© Jonathan Goldberg

Inside the Winter Gardens

opportunity of enjoying a very unusual experience. The Gallery, with views down through the foliage towards the paths and water below, provides opportunities to experience and possibly enjoy a dramatic sense of height and exposure.

© Jonathan Goldberg

Dramatic view into the Winter Gardens

Client's account

by Neil Sinclair, formerly Senior Curator, Sunderland Museum and Winter Gardens (Tyne and Wear Museums)

Sunderland Museum to 1995

Sunderland has the oldest publicly funded museum service outside London. In 1846, taking advantage of recently passed legislation, Sunderland Corporation took over the existing society-run museum. The first major public building erected by the council was the new Museum, Art Gallery, Public Library and Winter Gardens of 1879.

The site for the new building was an excellent one, as not only was it in Mowbray Park, Sunderland's main park, but it was also close to the developing town centre. The architects selected to design the building were J and T Tillman, who used a combination of their own version of French Chateau and classical Roman styles. Sir Nicholas Pevsner described it as 'hardly one of the ornaments of the Victorian period' in his *County Durham* volume of the *Buildings of England*. It is, nevertheless, an imposing structure and has become the best-loved public building in Sunderland since the demolition of the Victorian Town Hall in 1970.

The building soon became over-crowded and various schemes for its extension were put forward from the 1900s. It was, however, only in 1964 that a major extension, designed by the Borough Architect, was opened on the site of the Winter Gardens which had been destroyed following bomb damage in 1941.

By the 1970s, the building was once again extremely over-crowded, with both the Museum, now part of Tyne and Wear Museums (TWMs), and the Sunderland Central Library lacking space to develop their services. A solution to the problem came in 1995 when the Library moved into new premises in a converted department store on the opposite side of the road.

After a debate within Sunderland City Council, it was decided that all the vacant space should be allocated to the Museum. The Council recognised the significance of the Museum to the local community and the role it and other cultural facilities could play in the regeneration of the city. The establishment of the HLF also now offered the opportunity of substantial funding for the development of the Museum.

The aims of the project

Before the Museum gained control of the whole building, it had consulted its visitors about the aims of the development project. This was through annual visitor surveys and specific questionnaires that asked visitors to indicate what they felt were the most important of a range of possible improvements. The Education Officer also organised consultation meetings with representative groups of visitors with a wide range of disabilities.

Better access and public facilities came at the top of all visitors' lists. This reinforced the views of the staff, who were conscious that having a main entrance with steep steps, with access for wheelchair users and parents with baby buggies via a ramp at the rear of the building and ringing a bell for entry, was unsatisfactory. For those who could not climb the stairs to reach the upper floors, the goods lift had to be used. There was only one public toilet and a very small café on the second floor.

Sunderland Museum has had a long history of working with disabled people, starting with work with blind people in the early 1900s. Developing access to all groups, including projects with disabled people, became an important part of the Museum's agenda in the 1980s and 1990s. Sunderland Museum won several awards for access, in spite of its poor physical facilities.

The development project offered the opportunity to provide first class access; this was stressed in the submission to the HLF in 1996, when the first two objectives of the scheme were set out as being to provide a new level entrance and to improve access inside the Museum. The need to meet the requirements of the DDA 1995 was stressed. The other objectives included improving visitor facilities such as toilets, shop, café and education area, replacing life-expired electrical, heating, ventilation and security systems, and providing new displays with interactive exhibits and new storage areas and environmental monitoring.

The HLF awarded a 75 per cent grant for the project in 1997 under the Major Museums Programme. The initial plans for the Museum were, however, revised after the HLF made a later grant under the Urban Parks Programme for the refurbishment of Mowbray Park and the construction of new Winter Gardens. It made sense for the Winter Gardens to be constructed at the east end of the Museum, as both projects could share the same visitor facilities. Linking the two schemes would also lead to the creation of a major regional visitor attraction.

The project team

The team that carried through the project included members of TWM staff and, after the Winter Gardens became part of the scheme, members of the Sunderland City Contracting Services staff. Project management was provided by Turner and Townsend, architectural services by the City of Sunderland, gallery design by Redman Design, and access consultancy by Burdus Access Management. There was a monthly meeting of the team with the HLF's monitor, and regular meetings of the building design team and the teams of TWM's curatorial, education and conservation staff who were working with the designers on the individual galleries.

The City of Sunderland architectural section was appointed for the building design because of its involvement with the Museum over many years. Turner and Townsend and Redman Design were appointed after competitive interviews, and Burdus Access Management were engaged following previous work on other TWM projects.

It is important in any major museum development that the members of the project team work closely together. In Sunderland, the architect and display designer successfully coordinated their elements of the project. It was also beneficial that both were sympathetic to the access requirements.

Members of the museum staff were active participants in the design team, and found working with consultants with a wide variety of skills a stimulating experience. In conjunction with the clerk of works, it was also important to check that the building work had been carried out exactly as the plans specified.

The access developments

The decision to build a new level entrance at the west end of the building was one of the earliest taken by the Museum and was included in the architectural brief. Instead of the steep steps at the front of the building and the 'back door' entrance with ramp, there would be one level entrance for all, which would also be an architectural feature prominently visible from Sunderland's main street. The brief stated that the entrance should be in contemporary style, but should complement the Victorian Grade II listed building.

The Museum remained committed to the new entrance in spite of opposition from some councillors to closing the old, main, stepped entrance to the public. The Royal Fine Art Commission also queried this and suggested a ramp to the Victorian entrance; this would, in fact, have been very visually intrusive as well as involving a very long ramp. English Heritage supported the new level entrance and it was agreed at a full meeting of Sunderland City Council.

There were also physical problems in erecting the new entrance because its site was occupied by underground public toilets and an electricity sub-station. These had to be removed, the pavement re-graded at the entrance and a drop-off point built for minibuses used by groups of disabled visitors.

A further issue was the need to provide orange badge parking space close to the entrance. The highways engineers initially argued that there were enough marked spaces nearby, but after discussion agreed to provide four new bays directly opposite the new entrance.

While the new entrance took up much time in discussions with external bodies, the detailed designs for the interior of the building and the displays were being drawn up. To reinforce the Museum's brief, the access consultant produced a very comprehensive set of proposals for the project. While the vast majority were implemented, a few were dropped after the tenders came in over the scheme's budget, and reductions had to be made on all aspects of the construction budget. It was at this stage that the consultation undertaken with the representative groups of disabled people proved particularly valuable, as it had distinguished between what users felt to be essential for access and what they saw as more peripheral.

The improvements achieved included all public doors being either automatic or operated by push pads, and a lift serving all levels. The main public toilets were on the ground floor, where a family toilet and baby-changing facilities adjacent to the café were also situated. Additional accessible toilets were provided on all the other floors. The importance of adequate seating was recognised in both the circulation areas and the galleries.

An unexpected combination of exhibits near the main entrance

A new shop with a dropped section of counter was installed at the entrance, and a café created with views into the Winter Gardens. Much thought was given to the directional signage system inside and outside the building; this was supplemented by TV screens providing information on events in the Museum. In the eight new galleries, clear and legible text on the panels and labels was seen as a priority. All had 'hands-on' and computer-interactive features, while several also had audiovisual programmes with subtitles and induction loops.

The Museum in use

The Museum re-opened in July 2001 and was almost overwhelmed by 272,000 visitors in the first six weeks. This had the advantage of testing all the building's services. There were inevitably teething problems with some features such as lifts, but these were later resolved. Most of the access features have worked well. Only the signage has been less than fully effective, but sheet floor plans are now provided to supplement this.

The total of a million visitors was achieved in November 2003. Just as important as the visitor total has been public reaction. The quality of

the architecture and displays has been commented on, and the Museum's visitor comments book has shown that the access improvements have been particularly welcome. The new level entrance has proved particularly successful and one survey showed that no less than 10 per cent of visitors were either wheelchair users or carers with baby buggies, and in the first four months after opening, groups of disabled people made up 40 per cent of the total group visits.

Diane Gallinger of Jordan Heritage Resources, a Canadian museum access specialist, visited Sunderland in September 2003. In *Opportunities for Excellence: what Canadian museums can learn about disability access from outstanding British models*, a report for the Canadian Museums Association and the Department of Canadian Heritage, she wrote:

'One of the most emotionally satisfying afternoons during my seven-week tour was spent simply observing how people used the galleries and amenities at the Sunderland Museum and Winter Gardens. I was amazed to see the number of people with visible disabilities (let alone people with invisible disabilities that I could not detect) who felt free to drop in as casual visitors to the museum. In my experience of Canadian museums, I have never seen such a thing.

Several wheelchair users enjoyed meeting family and friends for lunch in the restaurant. A gentleman with a white cane came by with a carer to experience the galleries. A group of seniors – some wheelchair users, and some with intellectual disabilities – dropped by with their care givers from a nearby residential home without having to pre-book, and enjoyed a lively but relaxed afternoon visit to the textile gallery.

Sunderland summed up for me everything that we should be striving for in making museums accessible, namely creating a welcoming community space where people with all kinds of disabilities participate as freely, as fully and as openly as anyone else in society.'

For everyone involved in developing and delivering the improvements to Sunderland Museum, this was very much our ambition, and it is very rewarding to see it recognised and acknowledged by others.

Access consultant's view

by Steve Hudson, formerly Project Consultant, Burdus Access Management[1]

The background

Appointment of Burdus Access Management as access consultants to the Sunderland Museum and Art Gallery continued through May 1997 to December 1997, following the earlier involvement of David Burdus Associates in an application to the HLF for funding. This appointment was intended to provide guidance and support to the design team through the development of the refurbishment scheme, from outline design, RIBA Stage C, through to the detailed design stage.

The city centre location of the building on a sloping site meant there were challenges in relation to people being able to approach and enter the building. Internally, there were some difficult changes in floor levels between the original Victorian building and the galleries

and office spaces added later across the entire south-facing rear of the building.

Early consideration was given to the provision of a new entrance at street level from the west side of the building, entering through the existing extension. The intended strategy, in keeping with the conservation requirements, was as far as possible to provide any structural changes within the 1960s extension, preserving the original Victorian elements.

At this time, the strategies employed were not in a direct response to the DDA 1995, which was still thought by many disabled activists to be like a dog without teeth. At Burdus, we believed that we could use this legislation to support our advice to the client on the need to consider provision of improved access, including auxiliary aids, and to avoid discrimination. There was a clear understanding with the client from the beginning that the intention was to provide accessibility to the building and facilities above and beyond the existing Building Regulations Approved Document M guidance, and the cost plan made some initial allowance for this.

Our approach as consultants to the project was intentionally holistic, to achieve improved accessibility to facilities and services for all potential users and staff, including parents with children, and people with physical, sensory or intellectual impairments. Although other design team members were unfamiliar with the involvement of an access consultant in the procurement process, they were generally receptive to advice, encouraged by the enthusiasm of TWM staff to provide inclusive facilities.

Project description

A series of meetings were held with the various design consultants and other design team members to identify existing and potential barriers. This included site meetings to review the physical barriers internally and externally, to further inform the cost plan in relation to potential solutions; desktop reviews of architects' proposals for access, internal circulation and location of facilities; meetings with the gallery designers to review their proposals for the internal layouts of individual gallery spaces; and meetings with building control officers and the local fire officer to consider issues relating to egress and provision of refuge areas. Feedback reports from these meetings were circulated to design team members and discussed at regular project reviews and separate design team meetings.

Opportunities for consultation with disabled people locally were an issue explored early in the process with the TWM learning officers. This included meetings involving external organisations including Gateshead Council's Access to Information and Reader Services and three groups who were regular Museum users: Nookside Day Centre for adults with disabilities, Barbara Priestman School for children with physical disabilities and TEAM Wearside, a youth training scheme for young people with learning difficulties. The consultation with user groups clarified the principal concerns of current users and confirmed many of the recommendations that had been made.

Reference was also made to reports from an intellectual access audit of the Hancock Museum in 1996 prepared by Skills for People, Newcastle, and The Percy Hedley Centre. The audit had been based on a series of visits involving disabled children, teachers, speech and language therapists, as well as occupational and physiotherapists over a three-week period in February 1996. Many of the issues raised in relation to access into and around the building, and interpretation of exhibits, bore relevance to similar issues at Sunderland Museum.

Feedback from consultation with user groups confirmed the need to consider the use of appropriate finishes to provide slip-resistant floor surfaces, particularly in WC areas; signage with colour coding and tactile elements; seating for resting and viewing at appropriate heights for people with impaired mobility; the opportunity to move around freely without pushing doors open; a passenger lift large enough for wheelchair users to turn around in; plenty of 'hands-on' exhibits; a sanitary area with adult-sized changing bench and shower facilities, to avoid need for undressing, changing and cleaning on the toilet floor; the importance of communication aids and the need to advertise their availability. Later consultation by the project team was used to re-evaluate some of these issues in the light of budgetary constraints.

One issue that was identified by each of the organisations consulted with was the need for accessible and safe parking and a drop-off area close to the entrance. This was important for people arriving individually, and even more so for groups of disabled visitors who were reliant on assistance from the vehicle.

Feedback reports from consultation with user groups were circulated to design team members. A number of guidance documents were also specifically produced and provided to the design team including *Access – External and Internal Provisions*, *Guidance Notes on Lifts*, and *Notes on Fire Strategy*. These were based on the existing Building Regulations AD M, draft DETR guidance for use of tactile surfaces, JMU Technical Bulletins, as well as Burdus' experience of other projects and user consultation. TWM and their gallery designers Redman Design Associates were also advised to consider the provision of aids and equipment for educational use.

Options advised for consideration for assistance with orientation and wayfinding included the use of tactile guidance, LED lighting at floor level, electronic guidance systems such as talking signs and React speakers that respond to hand-held devices carried by users, as well as colour-coded and tactile signage.

Some of the options considered but later discounted for cost reasons, or which became unnecessary as a result of the design changes for the combined Museum and Winter Gardens Project, included: the use of power-operated sliding doors to accessible unisex toilets similar to those used on trains; a wheelchair platform lift on an existing steep internal ramp at third floor level, where it was considered prohibitively costly to remove the ramp and install a platform lift; an external vertical platform lift and enclosure at the east side of the museum to provide access for disabled staff and visitors from the on-site parking and drop-off point that existed prior to the Winter Gardens development.

Consultation with Museum users

While our involvement as access consultants on the project was relatively short lived, it is satisfying to see the success the project team have achieved, in particular the diligence of the TWM staff in adopting an inclusive approach and the designers' skills in providing responsive and sometimes innovative solutions. As well as achieving physical improvements to accessibility, a cultural change is in evidence. Sunderland Museum does not have 'disabled' facilities; it has accessible facilities. Educating minds and attitudes has been as important as converting the original buildings and site.

Consultation with the Museum users

by Jo Cunningham, Learning Officer, Sunderland Museum and Winter Gardens

The benefits of consultation

The Sunderland Museum development scheme provided ample evidence of the value of consultation in improving communication between the users and those in charge of buildings and budgets. Areas of priority for disabled people are highlighted and compromises can be agreed, or at least discussion can take place to which all parties can contribute. Professionals and users can gain a better understanding of each other's needs, removing assumptions and guesswork from the design process.

Bringing together disabled people who have different needs allows a broader consideration of access issues. The needs of disabled people are as individual as they are. A heightened awareness of this meant that no single area of access dominated the discussions.

The Museum and Winter Gardens today

The lasting benefits of creating an accessible facility can be measured in terms of visitor numbers. During its first year, Sunderland Museum and Winter Gardens attracted over 620,000 individual visits, and the proportion of groups identifying themselves as having special needs was 36 per cent of the total number of groups. The new facilities encourage visits not only by disabled people, but also by their

families, friends and from many other people such as families with young children and those whose mobility or eyesight is impaired through old age.

Improvements in access continue to be important. The education programme is varied and provides opportunities for all visitors to take part. Guided tours are arranged for groups of visually impaired people. Talks and demonstrations can be translated for BSL users by prior arrangement and all new temporary exhibitions have hands-on exhibits, large print versions of the labels and panel texts or sound guides as part of the interpretation. Disability equality training is compulsory for all TWM staff and is organised as a rolling programme to keep everyone up-to-date.

As well as maintaining good links with the three organisations originally involved in this consultation, TWM has established a Museums and Galleries Disabled Access Group, a panel of disabled people who meet regularly to review the facilities and services provided by TWM at various venues and through the internet. This continued dialogue keeps TWM informed of the views of disabled visitors, and helps to evaluate current practice and test new ideas.

Hands-on exhibits

Architect's account

by Michael Glen, Senior Architect, City of Sunderland

Appointment

Historically, TWM has appointed consultants from the in-house teams of the metropolitan authorities that make up the old Tyne and Wear County Council area. When Sunderland Museum wished to progress its HLF bid, this arrangement was continued, and the Museum asked the City of Sunderland's architects to develop the proposals. The City also provided structural and electrical engineering services and quantity surveying, while T and G Armstrong were appointed to carry out mechanical services design. Redman Design was appointed to design the museum displays and interiors.

While the City's architects had a long history of working at Sunderland Museum, at the time of the appointment the in-house services were being re-organised, and the client–architect relationship was a new one at the commencement of the project.

Client's brief

The client provided a detailed, 30-page brief at the start of the project. Accessibility was a central theme of the brief, and the client had already made the decision that an entrance to the building in a new location was essential, and that as many of the Museum's facilities as possible should be accessible to all. The client had carried out access surveys and engaged an access consultant who was to work with the design team.

The project had been advanced almost to the end of RIBA Stage C, Outline Design, when the brief was revised to make allowance for the new Winter Gardens, which were to form an extension to the Museum. A separate design team was appointed for the Winter Gardens, the result of an architectural competition, and the client team was also expanded. An independent project manager was appointed to oversee the complete development.

Access challenges

The first challenge was that of winning hearts and minds over to the idea of abandoning the original Museum entrance. The client was convinced of the need for this, but there was opposition from other quarters. There is undoubtedly a strong urban design argument for keeping original entrances in use, whenever practicable, to prevent streets losing their vitality, as buildings 'turn their back' on them. The Sunderland Museum was the major presence in Borough Road, but the benefits of a new entrance were, in this case, overwhelming. Drawings were prepared to illustrate a ramped access to the existing entrance, but the scale and size of the ramps radically altered the proportions of the classical elevation. The location selected for the new entrance was at a point where the external ground level was closest to street level, and was also a more prominent position in relation to Sunderland's busiest streets.

One consequence of the revised entrance location was the need to de-emphasise the original entrance. Various features and signage options were considered, but in the event, the conspicuous design and location of the new entrance means the majority of visitors have no problem coming to the right place.

Perhaps the greatest challenge to making the whole building accessible was the multitude of levels within the existing structure. The original Victorian (1879) building has two principal floor levels, ground and first, and a small second floor under the central dome, originally housing a caretaker's flat, but now housing part of the Museum's collection. The 1964 extension to the Museum connected at the same level at ground floor, but at an intermediate landing level of the 1879 building at first floor, and then introduced a second floor of galleries. The extension also contained an area of office accommodation where a second and third floor fitted into the storey height of the second floor galleries. Both buildings have basements at different levels. In total, there were nine different floor levels to be made accessible. The brief required wheelchair access to all these levels.

The solution to accessing the various levels also had to take account of the fire strategy for the building, which called for a fire escape lift serving the publicly accessible floors, with the appropriate refuges, a fire fighting stair and the necessary compartmentalisation of the building.

Another difficulty was the requirement for level access in the new main entrance. While the external ground level was higher here than

Conspicuous design of the new entrance at the west end

around the original entrance, with its flight of stone steps, there was still a half-metre rise to the Museum's ground floor level, and only limited pavement space for ramping up.

Design development

The client encouraged the project team, throughout the design process, to achieve inclusive solutions to all access issues. Wherever possible, inclusive facilities were provided rather than separate facilities for disabled people. The Museum's education staff and the project architect carried out consultations with local user groups with disabled members, to test proposed solutions and receive practical advice.

The design based on the original brief was a relatively conservative scheme which sought to provide improved circulation largely within the constraints of the existing structure. With the introduction of the new Winter Gardens proposal at the opposite end of the building to the new entrance, the concept of a multi-storey open space or 'Street' began to emerge. This was created between the 1879 and 1964 buildings by selective demolition, and it

formed a central orientation space as well as a route through to the Winter Gardens.

The junction between the 1879 building and the 1964 extension was architecturally unsympathetic, and it was felt that the newly created space between the two would improve this, and might also reveal evidence of where the original Winter Gardens had been attached to the 1879 building.

The client and display designers, while keen on the orientation possibilities of the Street, were concerned at loss of floor space and light intrusion into the galleries. After much discussion, the Street concept was carried out, but to only one-storey height for the first half of its length, opening out to the full height of the building, with a glazed roof, as it approached the new Winter Gardens.

In practice, the design has worked well, providing an easily identifiable layout to the public spaces, compared to the original design, in which the layout had remained quite convoluted. Traces of the old Winter Gardens were in fact discovered and remain visible in the completed project.

© Jonathan Goldberg

Museum Street at the Winter Gardens end

The various level differences throughout the building were overcome with a series of lifts, platform lifts, new and rebuilt ramps and new staircases. The central passenger lift, also a fire escape lift, was the most difficult to incorporate. Structurally, it was a tight fit within the reinforced concrete frame of the 1964 building, and required doors opening to landings in two directions. The small rise from the first floor of the 1964 building to the first floor of the 1879 building (approximately 1m) also had to be catered for in the lift design.

The lift engineers met these design requirements quite easily; however, there were teething problems in the initial operation.

A recurrent difficulty in the design process was reconciling the space standards required for wheelchair users and fire escape routes within the limitations of the existing structure, and demands on space for the galleries and displays. Three new staircases were required to provide adequate means of escape in the event of fire, two of which were within the existing building footprint. The cost of more major structural interventions precluded some solutions and compromises were inevitable in the size of spaces not dictated by regulation.

The problem of the level difference at the chosen location for the new entrance was overcome by building the entrance itself, reception and shop, at street level, and then introducing a 1:20 gradient to the first part of the new internal Museum Street.

The services of the access consultant were maintained up to RIBA Stage D of the project. The access consultant's input was, quite rightly, challenging, and the majority of the

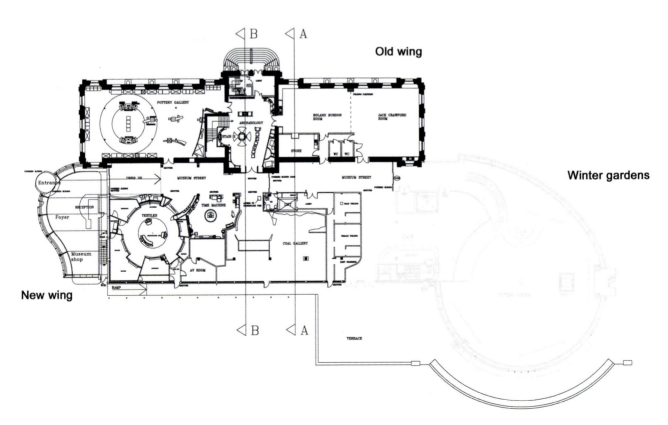

Ground floor plan

recommendations were taken on board. The attitude of the client and design team to the access issues was positive throughout. An example of one of the access consultant's recommendations that the design team was not able to achieve was for a covered area for transfer from a parked vehicle at the main entrance. Highways and planning considerations precluded such a solution with the entrance adjacent to a busy road junction. A canopy was provided, however, with a designated drop-off area within 15m.

Reducing barriers to movement through the building was achieved with powered sliding doors to the main route through the Museum Street and powered swing-doors to galleries, fire lobbies and toilets. Where possible, no doors were fitted at the entrances to galleries, or else doors were kept open with electro-magnetic devices. A number of original, very large, Victorian panelled doors were successfully changed to powered opening, and upgraded for fire resistance.

The importance of well-designed and readily accessible toilet facilities was stressed in the brief. A main facility was provided on the ground floor, together with a separate 'family toilet' and an accessible baby-change and feeding room. Accessible unisex toilets were provided in public areas at the other levels, including one equipped with a Closomat WC.

The problem of natural light intrusion from the roof glazing of the Museum Street into those galleries with light sensitive artefacts was largely overcome by the display designers. Deeper entrances were designed and sensitive artefacts placed further into each gallery. This also provided an interesting introduction to the galleries and gave time for eyes to adjust to the lower light levels.

One of the principal rooms in the 1879 building was designed as an education space for schools and user groups. This was provided with its own accessible toilet and storage facilities, and considerable attention was paid to acoustic performance, with absorbent wall finishes specified to reduce reverberation times.

The brief required that staff areas generally, and certain areas of the museums stores, be accessible to wheelchair users. This was achieved by incorporating platform lifts and powered door operators.

Project outcome

During work on site, the construction team ran into the usual problems inherent in existing buildings, especially to be expected in a building with a complicated history such as Sunderland Museum. Understanding the design of the concrete structural frame of the 1960s building, and how this connected to the 1879 building, was particularly problematic, and some of the solutions that looked feasible at design stage had to be somewhat modified on site to adapt to as-found conditions. Fortunately, no features critical to the functionality of the scheme were compromised.

A knock-on effect of additional work on the structure of the building was cost savings, which reduced the level of specification possible in certain areas. In general, successful compromises were found and the final scheme has a satisfactory feel of quality commensurate with its standing as an important public building. In terms of accessibility, the vast majority of the project's targets were met and the response of users has been very positive.

Update

by Helen White, Senior Manager, Sunderland Museum and Winter Gardens

Sunderland Museum and Winter Gardens continues to attract more than 300,000 visits a year, and has earned many accolades for the accessibility of its facilities and services, including praise for the positive attitudes of its front-of-house staff. In May 2004, Sunderland Museum and Winter Gardens was runner-up to the Natural History Museum, London, in the Visit Britain Excellence in England Awards, for Large Visitor Attraction of the Year. As described by Jo Cunningham in the section on consultation with museum users, improvements have continued to be made in response to observations by visitors and staff. The Museums and Galleries Disabled Access Group, formed of users and activists, together with TWM's cross-departmental Access Working Party, provides ongoing advice on policy and best practice to ensure that the building and its operation remain at the forefront of accessible museum provision.

View of Fisheries Museum from across the harbour

The Scottish Fisheries Museum, Anstruther, Fife

Overview

by Adrian Cave

The Fife Fisheries Museum was an early and innovative project carried out before the publication of Approved Document Part M, 1999 edition, and before the publication of BS 8300 in 2001. The significance of the project is that it illustrates how much can be achieved with limited funding but with enthusiasm, persistence and teamwork.

The scheme is designed within a complex group of small, historic buildings with many internal changes of level. The scope for access improvements was limited due to the constraints of the buildings and the severe limitations of funding for the project. The work was carried out in phases, and the main feature of the project from the access point of view is a very complex series of ramps following a sequential route through the buildings.

The result is a scheme that is accessible to most people, but wheelchair users are likely to need assistance because of the long and steep ramps. The Museum has a very informal atmosphere with a wide range of exhibits, and the character of the old buildings adds much to the experience of the visit to the Museum. The Museum provides for very informative and stimulating visits, including for children.

Given the constraints of the site and the limited budget, it is arguable that access via a steep ramp is better than no ramp. Therefore,

the building is accessible to all with assistance, but this could be improved by the following:

- more handrails
- improved illumination in some areas
- upgrading of the existing WC
- improved handrails to the front ramp and steps
- information in alternative formats

However, visiting the Museum gives a strong sense of the history of the fishing industry in this area, and includes buildings and boats which are a real part of life at this part of the Scottish coast. The Museum was established before the recent dramatic decline in the local fishing industry. This is not, therefore, a sanitised version served in a modern showcase, but a very informative illustration of life in the fishing industry in one of its original settings.

Fishing boats at the Fisheries Museum

Client's account

by J K Lindsay, General Manager

Introduction

Any examination of the problems encountered in the adaptation of old buildings for museum use, especially when the client is an impoverished, independent museum trust, would profit from a study of the redevelopment of the Scottish Fisheries Museum at Anstruther. The problem at Anstruther has been to take a heterogeneous group of separate but adjacent buildings of fine heritage quality, but in many ways structurally unsuited to museum use, and to link them together in such a way as to enhance the visitor experience for all, including those visitors with mobility difficulties. In addition, given the relatively low turnover each year, the entire project had to be completed in a staged programme at a modest cost and with an eye constantly on the trust's cash flow situation.

The museum is housed in a diverse collection of buildings facing the harbour at the foot of the 10m raised beach. The location once belonged to the Cistercian Abbey of Balmerino in North Fife, and the Chapel of St Ayles still stood on the site until circa 1850. In 1969, when the museum opened following sale of the site by the last fishing industry users, the property comprised the mid-16th century Abbot's Lodging; a merchant's house dated 1721; and various 19th century storehouses all arranged around an enclosed courtyard. All these buildings were A listed. Two adjacent B listed 19th century terraced houses with a smokehouse were added in the 1980s, giving a plan view resembling a number nine lying on its side, with the long axis to the landward side (see plan p 95).

The Museum buildings, seen looking north from the harbour, after redevelopment

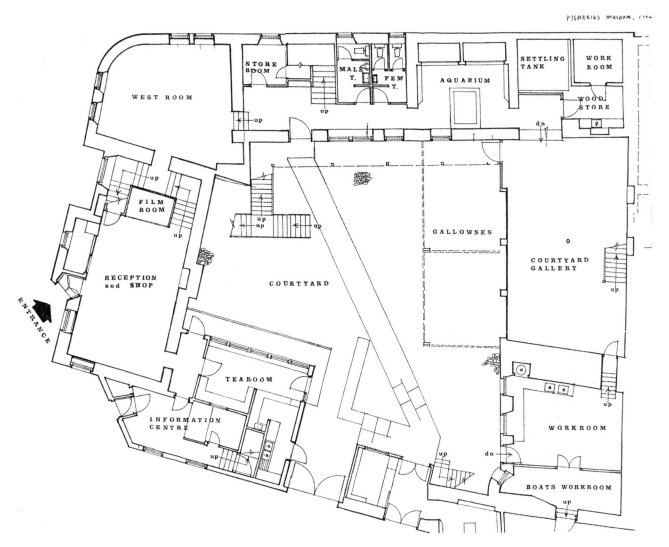

Plan showing the range of buildings before redevelopment

Objectives

A period of steady expansion over the first 15 years had been followed by five lean years, and in 1989, the Trust appointed a new general manager with a view to strengthening financial performance, which was seen as critically dependent upon improving the visitor experience at the museum. Some consultancy work had been carried out in previous years, with a view to improving the entrance, shop and tearoom facilities; but the estimated costs were substantial and the proposals did not find favour. Nor were the displays in the best of order. The buildings were domestic in scale with the displays in a series of separate, usually small, rooms. Given that these were in separate buildings, the path through the museum required visitors to retrace their steps at a number of points with consequent potential for confusion and even congestion at certain points on busy summer days. A chronological presentation of the Scottish fishing industry

was virtually impossible. The addition of the two terraced houses, while solving many of the previous storage problems, perpetuated this piecemeal aspect with the creation of a final cul de sac at the end of the tour. The other outstanding problem was the presence of a small aquarium inside the museum, which complicated the problems of controlling relative humidity in a seaside location, and which compared unfavourably with larger, more professionally run aquaria in St Andrews and North Queensferry.

A review of the situation in 1989/90 was entrusted to a team of four[2] (our architect, a board member and the General Manager, later joined by the new Curator) on the basis that

2 Walter Flett Faulds, Architect, Pittenweem
Dr R G W Prescott, University of St Andrews
J K Lindsay, General Manager
M Tanner, Curator

Aerial sketch of the group of Museum buildings

the board had a healthy suspicion of consultants, a very unhealthy cash flow, and in reality, who knew the museum better than our own people? It was soon agreed that we needed to create a one-way circuit for visitors (no cul de sacs) that followed the chronological sequence from prehistoric to modern times and that, given the current emphasis on facilities for disabled people, provision of these should be our guiding rule. In addition, the necessary improvements to the small tearoom, miniscule kitchen and entrance/shop (in the wrong place and too small) were to be taken into account, not forgetting to provide a new home for the Tourist Information Centre (TIC) which we accommodated (and which paid us rent!). Finally, given our delicate financial state, it would be more than slightly useful to keep all aspects of the museum at least partly operational while the work was in progress.

From the entrance pavement to the highest point in the museum, there were 18 levels to be linked. We did not wish to use lifts, due to bad experiences with these elsewhere, and the need to accommodate their machinery into an already crowded site. There were five existing sets of stairs, two of which had to be retained as the historical entrance to the Abbot's Lodging and an internal stair within, which linked the displays of a fisherman's home with the net loft above. Perhaps an audiovisual display could cover these galleries for wheelchair visitors? Linking many of the more modest of the remaining 15 changes of level had obvious solutions, indeed within our in-house capability, but in others, even the initial measuring of wall thicknesses and levels in adjacent, but unconnected, buildings was difficult. The insertion of metre-wide ramps into small rooms meant less room for display cases – the rooms often became the display case. Some ramps required railings – could these become part of the display material, and still remain usable? Using different materials to suit the context, they did. We learned too that space required for the ramps was not all lost. There were gains where stairwells were removed; some ramps were high enough to permit displays, or at least storage below. By the end of the project we reckoned to have gained eight per cent of usable space in the museum.

Programme

By May 1990, we had obtained endorsement for a project, estimated at £230,000 – a formidable sum for an organisation struggling at the time to improve an annual income of £67,000 – and were putting together a fundraising group from within our own board, with additional friends from outside. As summer visitors provided the bulk of our income, the work was divided into five sub-contracts or phases, with the first three scheduled for completion in time to open for public access by Good Friday 1991.

Parochialism, something of an art form in East Fife, raised its head at this point. Memories of the financial costs of having used contractors from outside the area were still fresh, but while there were a reasonable number of local firms, these were generally small and some had direct involvement in the museum board. The resultant need to strike a balance between competitive tendering and local prejudice was to prove a continuing thorn in the flesh of the architect, albeit the worst of the blood-letting was over the allocation of these early contracts.

Building alterations

Closure of the aquarium provided temporary storage, and Phase III was begun almost immediately since it did not impinge on the public areas. This involved the digging out of the long, narrow back court behind the terraced houses down to ground level in the gallery to the east side of the courtyard to provide a ramp for the return route to the visitors' starting point. The concrete ramp thus created entered the older buildings at a point where one of the original staircases would be demolished, and the concrete was designed to terminate just inside the old wall where central heating pipes ran at right angles to it. We did not wish to lower these pipes and risk an air lock, so they were bridged with a light, metal plate and the ramp continued in wood in the ground floor display. We then realised that if, as intended, we built the ceiling over the ramp at this point level with the underside of the floor above, we would have insufficient headroom to meet statutory requirements. Answer: replace the square metre involved with 'steel plate'. The main concern in excavating down 2m beside the foundations of three-storey buildings was of course, stability, and it was necessary to build a metre-wide concrete buttress alongside the building as

digging proceeded, thereby creating a flat, stepped shelf beside the ramp. The area was roofed over with concrete beams (in case we should wish to build above at a later date) and the resulting tunnel painted white throughout. Phase III was now dubbed the 'Cresta Run'; and the shelf? – an ideal location for the safe display of our collection of small marine engines, in the right location ahead of the large engines display into which the ramp debouched.

While the development of the Cresta Run in the northeast corner was comparatively straightforward, those working at the northwest corner were experiencing heavier weather. The plan here was to replace the existing entrance staircase by a ramp which would obliterate a cellar/cupboard, be driven through a ground floor wall, follow the curvature of the northwest corner building as it rose to first floor level, then angle southwards through a second major wall into one of the main display galleries. Once visitors had viewed the sailing vessel displays there, they would exit by ramp over the lower displays to reach the highest level of the whole system (through the same two walls). This ramp was the only occasion on which the architect had to build outside the footprint of our original buildings (see photo below).

This was the area which had given the biggest headaches at the measuring and levelling stage; no design problems arose from that, but we were to hit the practical problem of breaching 18th century walls. The only dressed stones in the buildings were at the window

The Cresta Run ramp after completion, showing the buttress on which small engines are displayed, and the low ceiling height at the far end, as the ramp enters the building on the east side of the courtyard

The exit ramp from the northwest gallery. The point at which the ramp exits the gallery at the far end was the only place at which construction work was required outwith the envelope of the original building

a rising slope, using flat boards, with no camber to upset the pedestrian public, but with all four wheels on the deck for the wheelchairs. After a week of unparliamentary language, they did it – perfectly (see photos below).

Meanwhile, the Museum frontage was being transformed. We had taken the decision that it would not be practical to consider employment of staff requiring wheelchair facilities, although this could be possible for volunteers manning the shop or acting as guides (we had 60–80 volunteers and five staff). That decision allowed us to create a larger office at first floor level, accessed from the stone steps to the Abbot's Lodging, and situated above the new toilets and TIC (which was given separate access from the street and its own accessible toilet). The former office, originally accessed by a wooden stair above the kitchen, was converted for use by the Curator, with access from the main display level, and the offending stair was removed. In turn, that permitted enlargement of both kitchen and tearoom,

and door surrounds. All the walls were built of boulders from the foreshore. By definition, these were the hardest of (usually) rounded stones which had resisted further erosion, and their nature had dictated the very dimensions of the whole structure. No chance here of cutting neat apertures with a Stihl saw; it was multiple needles and Acrow props, and the very careful removal of sometimes sizable boulders, with the end result resembling a shell hole rather than a doorway.

The holes re-faced and the dust removed, the building of the ramps began. We knew that this was the section where it was most difficult to maintain the recommended 1:12 maximum slope. We had extended the low end of the ramp as far back as possible, and similarly the high end by cutting into the ceiling of a cupboard fortuitously below, but although we had to accept a short section of 1:11, this was not the real hold-up. Wheelchairs have four wheels, but generally no springs – we were asking the joiners to follow the curved wall on

The ramp approaching the northwest gallery: during construction (top), after completion (bottom). This was the only point in the entire project in which gradients of the new ramps exceeded 1:12 (here it was 1:11)

which absorbed the area previously used by the TIC. The large gateway providing the main entry to the courtyard was removed and the tiny entrance/shop was expanded into this area. We still had to allow for the occasional delivery and removal of large display items, so the front and rear doorways in the new shop were carefully aligned, the railing on the entrance ramp from street level was designed to be removable, and the shop/reception furniture in this area made mobile.

That left the niggling question of the first and second floors of the Abbot's Lodging (the southeast corner). The displays of a fisherman's house and net loft had always provided a suitable closure at the end of visits, despite being historically out of sequence, as it displayed material from the early 20th century (other displays at earlier points on the route through the museum brought the fishing story up to the present time). Wheelchair access was impossible, due to both the external stone fore-stairs and the internal wooden stair between floors; and the relationship between the two floor levels and that of the Age of Steam gallery next door could not have been worse – the implied horizontal extent of any

connecting ramp would be colossal. And yet an audiovisual solution could break down, and seemed a poor option compared with our other efforts. Could we create a window? There was a cupboard where a breakthrough might be made – it seemed possible to create a two-part window through which a wheelchair user in the Age of Steam gallery could look up into the loft and down into the room, and see a fair bit of each. But these were the oldest walls in the place – was the thickness really the 18–24 inches our measurements seemed to indicate? Wisely, we decided to probe through from inside the cupboard, no small exercise in itself. Result – three feet thick – pause. This would make little impact on the view of the attic, but constricted the sight line into the house enormously. However, the thickness of the wall was a bonus. It permitted the positioning of two wide mirrors at 45° top and bottom in the cupboard to give a view of the entire room, except the wall from which the viewer was looking; and that was solved via a third mirror on the far wall (unseen by pedestrian visitors). The result was a wheelchair-friendly solution that also placed the Abbot's Lodging displays in the correct historical sequence.

The main entrance, shop and tearoom after completion

The early 20th century fisher-house displayed in the 16th century Abbot's Lodging: the periscope mirrors which enable wheelchair users to view this display from the gallery to the north, beyond the fireplace wall, are in the press to the right of the hearth

Conclusions

We had been blessed in our choice of architect; the team had not fallen out (well, not much); the workforce had (largely) been inspired by what we were trying to achieve – but did it all work? We were visited by a lady who had handled one of our applications for grant aid, along with her chairperson – herself a wheelchair user. We took them round, fearful of the verdict on the three to four yards of steeper ramp. 'Don't worry', the chairperson said, 'It's in the mind really. People won't fall over backwards, they only fear they will. Stick a phone on the wall so they can ask for help' (We did and it is seldom used). We completed the circuit. The chairperson wished to go back through the system (we had not thought of *that*). On the way, her colleague confessed cheerfully that she had regarded the project as so complicated that it would never come to fruition. We returned to the top of the chicane – at which point the chairperson launched

herself full tilt down the steep section, ending up with a triumphant wheelie at the starting point. 'Great', she said.

We were breaking new ground in the museum world at that time, and achieved more than we realised. The one-way chronological route was hardly innovative, but it solved our existing display problem. Creating ramps was the open sesame to solving future difficulties. No more buggy parking problems while harassed parents carried wriggling toddlers; the arthritic elderly, too, were finding ramps easier to manage than steps; and always there was the delight of a new dimension as artefacts were seen from different heights and angles. In the following nine years, the museum saw two further massive extensions – a £750,000 doubling in size by creating a loop to include former boatyard premises along the street, turning the old figure nine into a squashed inverted U-shape; then a further purchase and incorporation of the Sun Tavern site to fill in the 'U' at a similar cost. Each had its problems, but the approach laid down in 1990/1991 continued to serve so well that when an Edinburgh disabled group visited, following completion of the Boatyard project, and we asked their Chairperson to highlight any faults, she said 'Well, there's a wee thing here, and a little thing there, but they're so trivial I would never have mentioned them, if you hadn't asked.'

The museum's development was recognised in various ways,[3] but the best reward by far is seeing the visitors' faces afterwards.

[3] 1992 Best long-established visitor attraction (Scottish Tourist Board
1994 Visit by Princess Royal
1997 Joint Second (Scottish Museum of the Year)
Special Award for access for the disabled 1991–97 (Society for the Interpretation of Britain's Heritage)
2000 return visit by Princess Royal
Highly commended (Scottish Museum of the Year)

Dulwich Picture Gallery: view of main gallery from extension

Dulwich Picture Gallery, London

Client:	Director, Dulwich Picture Gallery
Architect:	Rick Mather

Overview

by Adrian Cave, with acknowledgement to Desmond Shawe-Taylor, the former Director at the Gallery and to publications by Marcus Binney, Catherine Crane, Jonathan Glancey and others.

The brief

Dulwich Picture Gallery, England's first public art gallery, was founded by the terms of the will of the painter, Sir Francis Bourgeois, upon his death in 1811. Within days of his death, Sir John Soane, Bourgeois' friend, was commissioned to design a building to house his collection. There were subsequent major changes in 1884, 1910, 1938 and in 1952 after bomb damage.

Changing requirements at Dulwich, as at other museums and art galleries, led to demands for new spaces and facilities. The brief for the development was drawn up in 1994 to address the backlog of deficiencies in the building and facilities at the Gallery. These covered four main areas of concern: the poor state of preservation of the Soane building and its inability to house the collection properly; the lack of adequate and suitable picture and frame storage and behind the scenes facilities; the poor visitor services at the Gallery; and the complete absence of dedicated space for the Gallery's famous education work.

The master plan

Rick Mather was chosen as the architect because his original concept most obviously addressed the concerns of the Trustees. His design was driven by three overriding principles: that intervention on such a beautiful site should be kept to a minimum; that the Soane building should be enhanced and not challenged by any new building; and that the new design should stress the historical relationship with the Old College building. It is for this reason that Rick Mather planned the new building to lie along College Road. This would mark out the suggestion of a second quadrangle for the College, as Soane originally intended in his first designs for the College.

The new block is, therefore, shaped in order to follow the line of College Road, at the same time as lying parallel to the Gallery. In this way it corrects the alignment of the road and makes a rectangular quadrangle or garden in front of the Gallery.

The analysis by the architect of the brief for the extension almost halved the new spaces needed, by re-using parts of the existing buildings and by combining into one adaptable space the apparently separate provision for exhibition gallery, lecture theatre, dining hall and reception spaces.

With this reduction in volume, the architect was able to emphasise the individuality of John Soane's original building: 'The illusion is that the museum sits on the edge of the country, looking out over fields. We have put all the new buildings on the village side, leaving the extensive grounds free of development.'

The new buildings, which are single storey and almost no higher than the garden walls, are linked to the existing buildings with a fully glazed 'cloister'. Even this is made less intrusive by the use of rooflights which, by illuminating the flank wall of the cloister, almost eliminate reflection from the glass wall. The cloister is supported on elegant bronze columns and even the manifestation of the glazing is minimal. Instead of the standard provision of two bands, each 50mm deep, at heights of about 1000 and 1500mm, this consists only of a single line of film, 20mm deep, at a height of about 1200mm. Although there is no manifestation on the glass below this, the plinth below the glazing consists of large river-washed stones which indicate the circulation route very clearly. BS 8300:2001 states that 'Glazed screens, which give the illusion that there is unimpeded access at these points, can be hazardous and confusing for people with impaired vision' (9.1.5). The glazed screens at Dulwich appear to have caused very few

problems for visually impaired people, almost certainly because of the clarity with which the line of stones helps to define the edge of the route, making this is an interesting and possibly provocative way of minimising the need for manifestation.

The original main entrance to the picture gallery has three steps up, and this difference in height is dealt with neatly in the new scheme with a carpeted ramp, at a gradient of 1:18, to a new side entrance. There is no handrail and no upstand at either side of this ramp. Although one would expect that a handrail on each side would be helpful for many people, very few problems have been reported, and the design is successful in achieving a sense of transparency at the link between the cloister and the original buildings.

Only disabled visitors are able to use the car parking spaces close to the ramp – an example of positive discrimination. The entrance from this car park has a power-operated sliding door, activated by a push panel, to enable disabled people to enter the cloister and to reach the ramp.

Glazed screens in the cloister with minimal manifestation

© Jonathan Goldberg

Once inside the gallery, the reception desk at the top of the ramp is at a height of 1100mm, considerably higher than normally recommended for accessibility, but this is not significant because the signing-in forms are clipped to a board which visitors can use at any height they wish – wheelchair users tend to rest the board on the arm of the wheelchair. This is another example of an elegant way of solving a problem where all the furniture in the gallery is required to be as unobtrusive as possible.

The shop is in the bay of the original entrance and, with short desks and low surfaces, is usable by most people. Within the gallery spaces, traditional seats with arms are well distributed and well used. John Soane's famous lighting design, with rooflights which provide natural illumination without glare, has been upgraded to meet modern requirements for the conservation of art works and energy, but remains as successful as ever, with minimal problems of glare for visually impaired people.

The gallery floor of new oak boards is light in colour and assists in the distribution of light. All visitors, including disabled people, are now able to move easily throughout the gallery and to compare, in the words of a former director, the 'beer drinkers' (British and Dutch) on one side and the 'wine drinkers' (French, Italian and Spanish) on the other!

Other major changes include the remodelling of the exterior of the gallery, of which Soane's original design had been greatly altered during the ensuing 150 years, in order to eliminate windows on the east façade. This led to significant gains in security as well as emphasising the solid brick rhythm of the original design. When the new works were completed in the year 2000, much of the difficult and expensive work had been hidden behind the finished surfaces, concealing the amount of effort required to make this sophisticated and accessible scheme appear effortless.

© Jonathan Goldberg

Gallery visitors

The new extensions and restored conservatory at the Horniman Museum

The Horniman Museum and Gardens, London

Overview

by Adrian Cave

Introduction

The Horniman Museum, a Grade II Arts and Crafts listed building, was designed by Charles Harrison Townsend and opened in 1901 for the 'recreation, instruction and enjoyment' of the people. Over the course of the last century, the Horniman, like many museums, was developed in an ad hoc way, with facilities added to the original galleries as needs became apparent or funds available. This resulted in inadequate spaces, with problems of access between the original buildings and later additions.

Brief

The architects, Allies and Morrison, were appointed in 1998 to develop proposals to improve the facilities for visitors, for the display and conservation of sensitive museum objects, and to reinstate the legibility and integrity of the original buildings.

Lottery funding and a successful fundraising campaign made it possible for the Horniman to clear away the unsatisfactory extensions, and create in their place a new building that radically transforms the experience of the visitor to the museum. The most dramatic consequence of the new building is the complete re-orientation of the museum, so that it now connects directly with the

Gardens, thereby realising Frederick Horniman's original intention. The main entrance is now accessed from the Gardens and reinforced by the location of the café, which overlooks the 16 acres of gardens and parkland.

However, largely because of the steeply sloping site, the experience for disabled visitors arriving at the museum may not be easy. Instead of the steps up at the original entrance, the visitor now has step-free access via a long sloping pathway, which follows the natural gradient of the ground up to the new main entrance. There are seats along this pathway to provide resting places and, with a natural slope of about 1:12, it is not surprising that these seats appear to be much in demand. Having negotiated this route through the Gardens, the visitor arrives at the new main entrance, which is at the upper level of the

Original entrance from the street

107

two-storey extension to the museum. Adjacent to the entrance doors are the reception desk, café, shop and WCs, so that visitors are able to relax and to refresh themselves before or after embarking on a tour of the museum and its unique range of exhibits. The restored conservatory is nearby.

Public access and use

The new building increases the museum's space by about 50 per cent, providing new galleries as well as an education centre, a shop and café. Linked to the historic core, it simplifies circulation and provides access for disabled visitors.

The completed museum provides the public with new environmentally controlled galleries for the permanent musical instruments collection, as well as the capacity to accommodate large touring exhibitions, as well as less fragile objects that can be handled. The exhibition galleries are mostly below ground level, with carefully controlled light levels, but in the public spaces, natural light is introduced wherever possible, creating an open and welcoming atmosphere.

These improved facilities are for the first time fully accessible to all visitors, with ramps and a new lift providing connections between all levels.

Aquarium below ground level

National Gallery from Trafalgar Square

National Gallery, London

Overview

by Adrian Cave

The new entrance into the National Gallery provides step-free access for the first time into the main galleries, and does so from the recently pedestrianised Trafalgar Square. The new entrance is practical and convenient for visitors, and aesthetically successful in combining high quality traditional materials such as polished stone and marble with modern architectural detailing. However, these features alone do not explain the significance of the project in a study about making existing buildings accessible.

The true significance of the scheme lies in the way in which the original design concept for the National Gallery has been exploited and developed to produce spaces with entirely new qualities. The National Gallery is arranged around a central hall and a series of eight open courts. Each of these courts, surrounded by galleries and circulation spaces at first floor level, provides daylight to the service spaces below the galleries at ground floor level. The courts, therefore, have the potential to be used in new ways, provided that the need for daylighting at ground level can be dispensed with by, for example, relocating the ground floor accommodation elsewhere.

This was achieved by the acquisition of a building at the rear of the National Gallery. The acquisition has allowed the two courts on either side of the main entrance and the central rotunda to be incorporated into a new scheme for phased improvements to the access and circulation routes into and within the gallery. The East Wing entrance is the first phase of this scheme.

A common problem in museums and art galleries is how to enable visitors to know where they are within the building. If this cannot be resolved satisfactorily, then elaborate signage systems will be necessary. If the sequence of spaces can be legible, particularly with spaces which provide clear links between the upper and lower floor levels, then the need for elaborate signage is greatly reduced.

The new East Wing entrance meets admirably the requirement for legible space because the

West doorway unchanged

East doorway with step-free access

© The National Gallery, London

The new hallway and stair – the Walter and Leonore Annenberg Court

route from the entrance leads directly towards the inner court and the upper floor galleries.

From the point of view of inclusive access, disabled people can now enter the building by the same route as everyone else, without the need to negotiate the steps up to the main portico. Immediately inside the entrance, a lift provides access to the level of the internal courtyard, Annenberg Court. From here there is a choice of a lift or escalator to the upper floor galleries. The architects describe the enclosed courtyard as 'a place of orientation, a breathing space within the gallery circulation system'. It also enables everyone to enter and leave by the same routes and the sense of space and orientation will be further enhanced when the West Wing entrance is completed on the other side of the main portico, at a later phase in the project.

A comparison of the west doorway, unchanged and with steps, and the east doorway, with step-free access, illustrates how a radical architectural intervention can be visually successful.

Camden Arts Centre

Camden Arts Centre, London

Client:	Camden Arts Centre
Architect:	Tony Fretton Architects Ltd
Access Consultant:	Earnscliffe Davies Associates Ltd
Design team artists:	MUF

Overview

by Adrian Cave

Although many old museum buildings have been provided with a new entrance and extensions at the side, it is very unusual to provide a new entrance in a modern extension at the front of the building. At Camden Arts Centre, the original entrance was via symmetrical steps up to the galleries at upper floor level. The new extension adopts the principle of taking pressure off the historic spaces by providing a new entrance, but does so at the lower ground floor by exploiting the changes in level of the site.

There are two access routes from the steep road frontage into the Arts Centre: from the upper slope, the route has step-free access and is suitable for wheelchair users, with a push pad for a semi-automatic entry door. Although Approved Document M recommends that the controls for powered doors are set as far back as 1400mm from the leading edge of the door when fully open (para. 2.21 g), here the push pad is set at the side and only slightly forward of the closed door. This appears to be a very practical arrangement, allowing space for a wheelchair user to keep clear of the opening door, and an example of how it can be sensible to question published guidance.

From the lower slope, close to the main road and bus stops, the route is via steps with a central handrail only and no kerbs at the sides. The central handrail allows visitors the choice of using either hand and is an effective minimalist solution to the problem of providing unobtrusive handrails in sensitive settings. The external steps and the landscaping also introduce visitors to the innovative qualities of the design before they enter the Arts Centre.

The ground floor is minimalist and modern with lots of glass, white walls and ceilings. The new entrance enables the reception, shop, café, offices and workrooms to be provided at lower ground level, with internal stairs and a lift to the upper floor levels. Both the ground floor and the upper floor levels have large uncluttered spaces, but each with a very different character.

The upper floor has Victorian features, also mainly white, giving the interior of the building a sense of unity by the quality of the space and light at each of the two main levels.

The ground floor café leads into the garden where there are steep slopes upwards. A path from the half landing of the stair leads to the middle levels of the garden with attractive views up and down the slopes, but because the

Camden Arts Centre, London

Level access from upper slope

Stepped access from lower slope

Lower floor gallery

half landing could not reasonably be served by a lift, it was only possible to make this area accessible by stairs for ambulant people. However, the large terrace, level with the café, and extending across the whole of the garden, provides a place that people of all abilities can share. The lift between floors, also used for art transport, is very large and able to accommodate several wheelchair users at the same time.

The new ground floor spaces in the building are notable for a feeling of light and openness, and the large sheets of glass have only minimal manifestation. This appears to work well, mainly because the clarity of the circulation routes and the detailing help to make the windows visible. This project is important as a demonstration of how to make an old building more accessible in an uncompromisingly modern and minimalist style.

Terrace and café

Norton Priory, Runcorn

Norton Priory, Runcorn

Overview

by Adrian Cave

A flat-roofed, steel building provides an unexpected context for exploring the ancient remnants of Norton Priory. The design works because the building becomes an unobtrusive background to the richness of the medieval architecture and of the landscaped garden.

Funded and run by a small charity, Norton Priory is a most unusual combination of community activity, social participation, education and conservation. For many years, a key role in the life of the project has been performed by a local enterprise which provides care and services for people with learning difficulties, and which enables them to participate in the gardening and maintenance work at the Priory.

There are four significant obstacles to access for disabled people and, largely because of limited funding, these are dealt with for the time being by management arrangements rather than by physical alterations. These four obstacles are:

- The medieval undercroft to the Priory, which is the main surviving architectural feature of the monastic establishment, is difficult to reach for someone in a wheelchair, or for anyone who has difficulty in negotiating three entrance steps without handrails. However, a route for people with disabilities could be provided around the side and to the rear of the undercroft, without damage to the stonework foundations, possibly by using timber decking. This is a route which many people would find useful. Meanwhile, temporary ramps and the assistance of staff and volunteers can enable most people to have access to the undercroft.

- The Viewing Gallery, which provides views down on to the garden and to the foundations of the ruined building, can only be reached via a spiral staircase. A DVD film, which is proposed, would be of benefit to many people who had difficulty in reaching the Viewing Gallery.

- A front entrance door with a step up, for which a temporary ramp is used when necessary. When inspected, the bell was too high to be reached by a wheelchair user, but staff at the adjacent reception desk were able to see if someone needed assistance at the entrance door.

- A WC designed for disabled people is slightly too small and of an outdated design which does not allow adequate space for either lateral or frontal transfer from a wheelchair. An accessible WC to current standards could probably be provided within the space available.

Entrance area

The undercroft at Norton Priory

Norton Priory Map

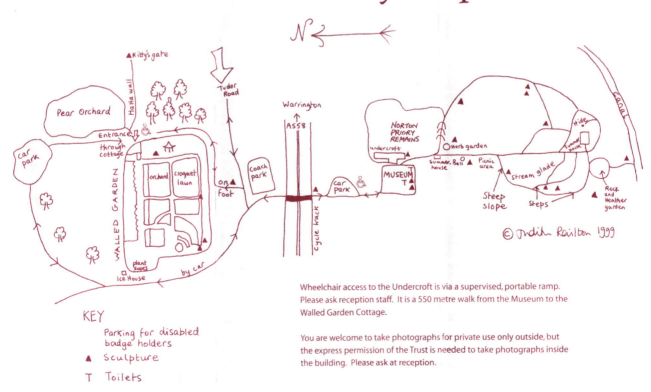

Wheelchair access to the Undercroft is via a supervised, portable ramp. Please ask reception staff. It is a 550 metre walk from the Museum to the Walled Garden Cottage.

You are welcome to take photographs for private use only outside, but the express permission of the Trust is needed to take photographs inside the building. Please ask at reception.

Site plan

Having entered by the front door to the Museum, the visitor has level access to the shop, café and museum, the latter with impressive displays of carved stonework, artefacts and reconstructions of the medieval Priory. Some of the displays include graphic explanations of medieval diseases and medicines. Others convey images of the life of the monastic community and of local people.

Externally, there are extensive routes without steps through the landscaped gardens which are meticulously maintained and cared for. Following the lie of the land, some slopes are steeper than 1:12, but most of these can be avoided, by studying the excellent, clear and very simple plans provided. Many people, both with and without disabilities, can derive pleasure from circulating through the gardens, enjoying the flowers, trees and shrubs, watching or listening to wild birds and seeing or hearing the water in the streams and the adjoining Bridgewater Canal.

At some distance from the main Priory, but with car parking nearby, the walled garden is rich with the sights, colour, shapes, texture, smells and sounds of insects, plants and foliage. The high stone and brick walls which surround the garden provide shelter and warmth for plants and visitors alike. Although entry via the Gardener's Cottage involves negotiating steps, there is level access nearby via a gate through the garden wall. The firm surfaces of rolled gravel or stone provide safe and easy access for a wheelchair user or anyone with a disability to enjoy this very unusual garden.

Norton Priory is a very attractive place to visit, both inside the buildings and in the gardens. When funds are available, a limited number of improvement works could make the museum and gardens more easily accessible to everyone.

Priory gardens

The entrance courtyard at Captain Cook Memorial Museum, Whitby

Captain Cook Memorial Museum, Whitby

Client:	Dr Sophie Forgan, Captain Cook Museum
Architect:	Clive Sheridan
Access Consultants:	Whitby Disabled Acceess Group

Overview

by Adrian Cave

This museum makes an interesting comparison with Norton Priory because both are run by small independent charities with very limited funds.

The advantages of making a new entrance when converting a small house to a museum are evident at the Captain Cook Memorial Museum at Whitby. The original entrance to the house was directly off a narrow cobbled street and, if this had been maintained for the Museum, it would have resulted in the main front room being used as the entrance and reception area. The arrangement adopted for the museum is that the entrance is made through a side passage into a courtyard which faces on to the harbour. As well as enabling the entrance and reception area to be provided in relatively unimportant spaces at the rear of the building, the entrance via the courtyard gives visitors a view of the harbour and permits the maritime setting to be experienced much more effectively than when entering from the street.

A stone ramp from the courtyard up to the entrance door has a gradient of about 1:13, but no handrails, so that there is a risk of people slipping on the stone surface, or falling

© Jonathan Goldberg

This ramp, without handrails, fits well into the stone courtyard. Even though it has no adjacent steps, handrails or a kerb, there have been no reported problems with access

THE HOUSE ON THE HARBOUR

Grape Lane was built on land reclaimed from the river in the 17th century. In 1649 staithes (or timber piles which also acted as a rough and ready wharf) were constructed here by Sir Hugh Cholmeley, the lord of the manor. Their purpose was to stabilise the river banks and prevent floods from damaging property on this side of the town. Once the land was stabilised, houses could be built.

The first house on this site was built in 1688 for Moses Dring, a mariner, and his wife Susannah. Their initials may still be seen on the front of the house. It was then bought by Captain John Walker in 1729, the father of the John Walker to whom Cook was apprenticed.

The site provided both a family home and the place from which the family shipping business was run. It would have looked very different when Cook knew it. The old kitchen wing of the house was still in place. There was a roughly cobbled slipway running down the centre of the yard to the harbour, which would have been useful for small boats loading materials. It was found lying a metre below the present surface of the yard.

The artist's impression shows how it may have looked at that time. The yard must often have been a scene of noise and activity. Young apprentices would have their first introduction here to the ships and the many tasks they needed to learn.

The present cottage wing of the house was built in several stages. In Cook's time it was a two-storey unheated building with a small annexe, used no doubt for stores and as a workshop for minor repairs.

It is not known when the kitchen wing was demolished. But the store was then doubled in size and a chimney added to create the cottage now seen here. At some stage the slipway was filled in. Gradually the site lost its close links to shipping and became simply a domestic dwelling.

The plants in the flowerbed have been chosen to reflect the domestic history of the site. All are varieties or species that would have been found in an 18th century garden.

The building and harbour in the 17th century

at the edge of the ramp. This is an example of a situation which should be monitored, so that a handrail and kerb could be fitted if there are problems.

A display panel in the courtyard includes drawings which show the building and the harbour as they might have been when Captain Cook was an apprentice and, because one of the first exhibits which the visitor sees is a globe with the routes of Captain Cook's voyages, the historical context of the museum is well displayed from the start.

Like Norton Priory, the Captain Cook Memorial Museum was established by a small charity with very limited funding, but this has been turned to advantage, by maintaining the intimate scale of the Museum with imaginative use of drawings, models and memorabilia. A lift, carefully concealed behind traditional doors, provides access from the ground floor to the first floor, enabling most of the exhibits to be seen by visitors who cannot use the stairs. However, the roof space where the apprentices slept can be reached only by a very steep staircase with limited headroom. No attempt has been made to change this unusual and atmospheric space but, instead, a DVD shown on a television set near the entrance gives

Steep steps to the roof space

© Jonathan Goldberg

Museum shop

everyone the chance to listen to a commentary about the life of Captain Cook. The quality of the exhibits and the intimate scale of the building help this small museum to convey the dramatic role of Whitby in the history of navigation and exploration.

The website, which is informative and easy to use, is an example of how a small museum can provide information and displays in ways which are truly accessible and inclusive, even though parts of the premises may be inaccessible.

© Jonathan Goldberg

Reception and shop

The central atrium at The Lighthouse, Glasgow

The Lighthouse, Glasgow

Client:	Glasgow 1999 Festival Company
Architects:	Page and Park
Access Consultants:	Tom Lister, JMU Access Partnership

Overview

by Adrian Cave

Located on a restricted site at the city centre, this project involves access issues which are very different from those in the other projects in this study. The original building consists of five storeys of level floor space, dating from 1895 and designed by Charles Rennie Mackintosh as the premises of the Glasgow Herald. Without improved access to the upper floors, the premises could not have been used as a museum and arts centre. The design solution, which allows the original buildings to be preserved almost intact, was to add a vertical extension which includes a reception area and shop at the ground floor, with lifts and links to all the main upper floor levels. The new extension follows the principle, adopted in other successful access improvement projects, of using an extension to take intrusive facilities and activities away from the historic areas of the premises.

This scheme has, therefore, a very clear concept of a new extension adjacent to the old building, in which the extension provides stair, lift and escalator access to all the upper floor levels. The central, vertical shaft through the full height of the building gives clarity to the circulation at all levels.

The clarity of the original concept is, however, marred by subsequent alterations by the building users.

- The reception desk is no longer suitable for wheelchair users.

- There is glare from exposed panels of vertical fluorescent tube lights, which is confusing for many people, particularly for anyone with impaired vision.

- The angled signpost shaft with irregular shelves and irregular signage is difficult to read and more confusing than helpful.

- Lettering and signage generally are often difficult to read except on the panels adjacent to the lift.

At the upper floor levels, circulation at each floor of the original building is clear and straightforward, including access to the conference room. However, the single lift, serving about six upper floors is not adequate for the demand, and this causes queuing and delays. In any case, a single lift is certain to be out of order from time to time. Two lifts would provide a more reliable service, which is essential for anyone who cannot manage the

View down the central, vertical shaft

The view through remotely controlled telescope at the Lighthouse

stairs. The provision of two lifts in fact had been considered, but was discounted by the client for space and cost reasons in favour of provision of escalators from the ground to the fifth floor. This responded to the challenge of attracting the public to a seven-storey-high public arts building.

The viewing platform at level six provides striking vistas over the local rooftops. Although there is no manifestation on the glass, this should not cause problems because the clarity of the large sill and the relatively close vertical mullions give a clear indication of the position of the windows.

The spiral staircase to the top of the water tower is too long and difficult for many people to use. Therefore the arrangement of a computer screen at level three, with a control panel to turn a camera at the top of the building and to zoom in and out for different views, is a very effective and interesting feature.

There are two open-riser stairs, one with an upstand above the treads of only 22mm, which

is confusing and inadequate, whereas the stair up to the water tower has upstands of 33mm above the treads. This appears to be more satisfactory, both for people with impaired vision and those who need to feel the riser with the front of a shoe.

The main staircase does not have good visibility for the treads, particularly when going down, because, although the treads are marked with stippled stonework, this has become dirty and provides very limited contrasts of colour and tone. This is a common problem because stippled stonework can appear to be very visible when new, but in buildings with high usage becomes less clear, unless cleaned regularly.

The project has been successful in transforming the former premises of Rennie Mackintosh's building for the Glasgow Herald into an arts centre which is used very intensively and for a wide range of activities. Some features of the new project such as the reception area, ground floor lighting, internal signage and the maintenance of the stairs have been changed in the years following the completion of the building works, with results which do not make life any easier for disabled people. The lesson from this is that inclusive design can only be sustained by inclusive management, in which the needs of all visitors, including those with disabilities, are fully understood and taken into account.

View of the Queen's Gallery from outside the Scottish Parliament

The Queen's Gallery, Edinburgh

Client:	Palace of Holyroodhouse
Architect:	Benjamin Tindall Architects
Access Consultant:	Tom Lister, JMU Access Partnership

Overview

by Adrian Cave

This is a gem, beautifully designed and constructed with first class materials and workmanship. The entrance into the Gallery is generous and welcoming with direct access to the reception desk and the lift, with the shop on the right. The exhibition is in two galleries upstairs which can be reached via the lift or a staircase. The glass double doors towards the stair have figurines placed on the horizontal bar of the door which act as door handles. The figures which people are most likely to hold near the leading edge of the door are smooth, and those with projections, such as a figure holding a book, are at the side. The doors are rather heavy to open, but staff are constantly available if anyone should need assistance. At the foot of the stairs there are computer screens which are generally accessible to disabled people and provide information about the museum and the exhibits.

The shop at ground level is very accessible with good illumination, and many objects are displayed at low level. There are only a few minor criticisms such as the coir matting inside the main entrance door and the door to the shop, but this is a very firm surface in both cases. A hook in the WC is at a high level, out of reach for someone in a wheelchair, but very unusually an alternative

hook is provided at a lower level. The locking latch is too high.

The staircase is constructed in timber with inlaid black nosing strips, which show up well. The timber handrail has a width of about

© Eva Zielinska-Millar

Staircase and balcony

© Eva Zielinska-Millar

Lighting in the gallery

© Eva Zielinska-Millar

Two heights at the reception desk at the Queen's Gallery enable a range of visitors to be attended to

120mm, considerably wider than normally recommended, but the lift is adjacent for those who would find the stair difficult.

The upper galleries in this former school are underneath a timber-framed and trompe-l'oeil timber ceiling, with a fine timber floor and deep timber skirtings. Lighting is well distributed without glare, and a combination of the lighting and the timber finishes contribute to a very comfortable environment in which to enjoy the paintings.

The balcony handrail is curved opposite the symmetrical staircase, and the resultant hallway, which extends from the ground floor to the upper floor, gives a very strong sense of location and of high quality materials within this small building.

Sources of useful information

Organisations

Centre for Accessible Environments
70 South Lambeth Road
London SW8 1RL
Tel/textphone: 020 7840 0125
Fax: 020 7840 5811
Email: info@cae.org.uk
Website: www.cae.org.uk

Provides technical information, training and consultancy on making buildings accessible to all users.

Department for Communities and Local Government
Eland House
Bressenden Place
London SW1E 5DU
Tel: 020 7944 4400
Fax: 020 7944 9645
Email: bregsb.br@communities.gsi.gov.uk
Website: www.dclg.gov.uk

For information on the Building Regulations in England and Wales.

Disability Rights Commission
DRC Helpline
Freepost MID 02164
Stratford-upon-Avon CV37 9BR
Tel: 08457 622 633
Textphone: 08457 622 644
Fax: 08457 778 878
Email: enquiry@drc-gb.org
Website: www.drc.org.uk

An independent body set up by the government to prevent discrimination against disabled people. Publishes codes of practice and other guidance related to the DDA.

The Equality Commission for Northern Ireland
Equality House
7–9 Shaftesbury Square
Belfast BT2 7DP
Tel: 028 90 500600
Fax: 028 90 248687
Textphone: 028 90 500589
Email: information@equalityni.org

Works towards the elimination of discrimination and keeps the relevant legislation under review.

Museums, Libraries and Archives Council
Victoria House
Southampton Row
London WC1B 4BE
Tel: 020 7273 1444
Fax: 020 7273 1404
Email: info@mla.gov.uk
Website: www.mla.gov.uk

National development agency working for and on behalf of museums, libraries and archives. Advises government on policy and priorities for the sector.

National Register of Access Consultants
70 South Lambeth Road
London SW8 1RL
Tel: 020 7735 7845
Fax: 020 7840 5811
SMS: 07921 700 098
Email: info@nrac.org.uk
Website: www.nrac.org.uk

Enables clients quickly and easily to locate suitable auditors and consultants, and provides a quality standard for those advising on the accessibility of the built environment for disabled people.

Royal Institute of British Architects
66 Portland Place
London W1B 1AD
Public information line: 0906 302 0400
Tel: 020 7580 5533
Fax: 020 7255 1541
Email: info@inst.riba.org
Website: www.architecture.com

The RIBA advances architecture by demonstrating benefit to society and excellence in the profession.

Scottish Building Standards Agency
Denholm House
Almondvale Business Park
Livingstone
West Lothian EH54 6GA
Tel: 01506 600 400?
Fax: 01506 600 401
Email: info@sbsa.gsi.gov.uk
Website: www.sbsa.gsi.gov.uk

For information on the Scottish Technical Standards.

Further reading

Legislation, standards and codes of practice

The Building Regulations 2000 Approved Document M: Access to and use of buildings (England and Wales)
NBS, 2006

The Building Regulations (Northern Ireland) 2000 Technical booklet R: Access and facilities for disabled people
Great Britain Department of Finance and Personnel (Northern Ireland)
The Stationery Office, 2001

Non-domestic Technical Handbook
Scottish Building Standards Agency, 2005

BS 8300:2001 (Incorporating Amendment No. 1) Design of buildings and their approaches to meet the needs of disabled people – Code of practice
British Standards Institution, 2001

A comprehensive best practice document, based on ergonomic research.

BS 5588:Part 8: Fire precautions in the design, construction and use of Buildings – Code of practice for means of escape for disabled people
British Standards Institution, 1999

BS 5588:Part 12: Managing Fire Safety
British Standards Institution, 2004
Designing, planning and management for means of escape for disabled people.

Code of Practice Rights of Access to Goods, Facilities, Services and Premises
Disability Rights Commission
The Stationery Office, 2002

The duty to promote Disability Equality: Statutory Code of Practice (England and Wales)
Disability Rights Commission, 2005

The duty to promote Disability Equality: Statutory Code of Practice (Scotland)
Disability Rights Commission, 2006

Other publications

Access for Disabled People to Arts Premises: The Journey Sequence
by C Wycliffe Noble and Geoffrey Lord
Architectural Press, 2004

Access to the Built Heritage – Technical Advice Note 7
Historic Scotland, 1996

Easy Access to Historic Buildings
English Heritage, 2004

Guidance in relation to achieving better access in historic buildings.

Easy Access to Historic Landscapes
English Heritage and Heritage Lottery Fund, 2005

Overcoming the Barriers – Providing Physical Access to Historic Buildings
CADW, 2002

Building Sight
by Peter Barker, Jon Barrick, Rod Wilson HMSO in association with the Royal National Institute of the Blind RNIB, 1995